THE GOD OF THE XHOSA

THE GOD OF THE XHOSA

A study of the origins and development of the traditional concepts of the supreme being

JANET HODGSON

OXFORD UNIVERSITY PRESS
CAPE TOWN

Oxford University Press

OXFORD   LONDON   GLASGOW
NEW YORK   TORONTO   MELBOURNE   WELLINGTON
NAIROBI   DAR ES SALAAM   CAPE TOWN
KUALA LUMPUR   SINGAPORE   HONG KONG   TOKYO
DELHI   BOMBAY   CALCUTTA   MADRAS   KARACHI

AND ASSOCIATES IN
BEIRUT BERLIN IBADAN MEXICO CITY NICOSIA

ISBN 0 19 570297 2

Printed and bound by Citadel Press, Lansdowne, Cape
Published by Oxford University Press, Harrington House,
Barrack Street, Cape Town 8001, South Africa

In memory
of
Professor Z. S. Qangule
scholar and friend

CONTENTS

Note on terms

It is appreciated that many terms used during the 19th century cause offence if used today. 'Kafir' (Kaffir) was the Arabic word for unbeliever or infidel and was commonly used by both black and white writers of the time when referring to black people, more especially those living on the Xhosa-Cape frontier. Their country was called 'Kafirland' or Kaffraria (Caffraria). These terms have had to be retained where necessary in quotations and of course they also feature in the titles of numerous books.

The use of the term 'traditional' in relation to the Nguni people is simply to indicate the state of these people and their beliefs before they were influenced by western culture.

Standard spellings for Xhosa terms are rare because they were spelled phonetically by the authors who recorded them. At times alternate spellings are given in brackets in order to avoid confusion.

Note on pronounciation of 'clicks'

For the Xhosa, 'c' represents the dental or front click, 'x' the lateral click, 'q' the top click.

For the Khoisan, as given by Schapera (1965, p. 421), '/' represents the dental click, '!' the palato-alveolare (or cerebral) click and '//' the lateral click.

ACKNOWLEDGEMENTS

It is with deep gratitude that I dedicate this work to the memory of Professor Z. S. Qangule, scholar and friend. Professor Qangule was born at Nqamakwe in the Transkei. After matriculating at the Blythswood Institute in 1955, he went on to gain a succession of degrees: B.A. through Rhodes University in 1960; U.E.D., B.Ed. and M.A. through the University of South Africa; and D.Phil. through the University of Cape Town in 1979. He came to the University of Fort Hare in 1974 as a lecturer in the Department of Xhosa and Sotho and was appointed to a professorship in 1980. Professor Qangule will be remembered for his valuable contribution to Xhosa literature, which includes poems, essays, a novel, a play and numerous translations from English into Xhosa; but above all he will be remembered for his profound humanity as a person. We began working together in 1978 and his enthusiastic interest in my studies on Xhosa traditional religion and the Xhosa prophet Ntsikana was always a great encouragement to me. I count it a privilege to have known him. Professor Qangule died on the 31st January 1982 at the age of forty-seven years. He will be sadly missed by his family, his colleagues, his students and his friends.

I owe a debt of gratitude to the many people who helped me during the four years that I have worked on the study of Xhosa myth and religious beliefs. In particular I would like to thank Professor J. S. Cumpsty of the Department of Religious Studies at the University of Cape Town, for his guidance and encouragement in researching and writing this work and for use of material from his article 'A Model of Religious Change', in *Religion in Southern Africa* 1 (2) July 1980; Father D. J. Dargie of Lumko Missiological Institute, Lady Frere, for his assistance with field work and with revising the manuscript; Dr J. Peires of the Department of History at Rhodes University, for his constructive criticism of the first draft; Mr M. Hirst of the Kaffrarian Museum, King William's Town, for his critical comments on the first draft and contributions on early Xhosa history and diviners; Professor H. W. Pahl, Director of the

Xhosa Dictionary Project, University of Fort Hare, and Father A. Fischer of McKay's Nek Mission in Transkei, for their suggestions concerning linguistic usage and general information; Professor E. J. de Jager for permission to use material from *Transition and Change in a Rural Community* (Fort Hare, 1972) by Professors E. J. de Jager and D. F. Raum; Mr G. Nkonki for permission to use material from his unpublished thesis, 'The Traditional Prose Literature of the Ngquika', and Mrs E. Pahl of Alice, for her assistance with editing the manuscript.

I am greatly indebted to those who so patiently gave me information during my field research: Chief S. M. Burns-Ncamashe, Father H. Kuckertz, Professor V. Z. Gitywa, Rev. C. C. M. D. Hoyana, Mr H. Nabe, the late Professor Z. S. Qangule, the late Mr A. M. S. Sityana, Mr B. Somhlahlo, the late Professor M. Wilson, and the students of the University of Fort Hare. My field work would not have been possible without the hospitality so graciously given by innumerable friends in Ciskei and Transkei, especially Dr E. Cundill and Mr and Mrs R. Raven of Alice, and the priests of the Catholic presbytery at King William's Town and Lumko Institute, Lady Frere. I would like to thank Mrs P. Newton for typing the manuscript twice over, Mrs K. Hingle of Oxford University Press for editing it, Miss Marlette Aucamp of the S.A. Library for compiling the index and Mr K. Behr for drawing the maps.

A special word of thanks must be given to my husband, John, my children, Michael, James, Alastair and Carol, and my parents, Mr and Mrs Harry Wood, for their constant encouragement and support which made this study possible.

I gratefully acknowledge financial assistance from the Harry Oppenheimer Institute for African Studies at the University of Cape Town and the Human Sciences Research Council.

The publication of this book would also not have been possible without the generous subvention from the Centre for African Studies, University of Cape Town.

Finally, I would like to add that the opinions expressed and conclusions reached in this book are the author's and are not to be regarded as those of any of the bodies mentioned.

PREFACE

In the Introduction to this book I have indicated some of the problems involved in trying to reconstruct Xhosa religious history, given the limitations of the primary material. The main difficulty is that most of the evidence of the early beliefs has of necessity to be inferred from later oral and written sources, and their bias and assumptions leave them wide open to criticism. Nonetheless, I believe that this study is a valid one because while it may not meet the priorities of an historian, it does seek to break new ground in the historical study of religion in Southern Africa and the priorities in this field are somewhat different.

The structure of the study speaks for itself. Part One provides an Introduction and Background to Xhosa history and society, more especially the interaction of the Xhosa with the Khoisan. The Second Part on Myth is divided into two sections, cosmogonic myths and myths about the coming of death. The four sections relating to the Supreme Being in Part Three are set out according to the different praise-names. I have specifically not separated the names of the supreme being from his functions and from Khoisan and missionary influences, and these from their context in ongoing Xhosa history, because I believe that it is precisely by looking at the inter-weaving of all these influences that patterns emerge which may be recognisably similar to those of other cultures and other times. My conclusions are therefore contained in Part Four.

I am not simply seeking to discover and record the facts of the past, nor do I believe that I will ever be in the position to say that this socio-cultural experience produced that modification in religious belief or that this religious belief produced that effect on society; but it is possible to discern patterns in relationships and when these recur, as for example the relationship between the symbol of transcendence and inability to affirm the texture of the contemporary socio-cultural context, one begins to look for these in appropriate contexts. I am well aware of the dangers of going into an historical situation with a model controlling one's expectations; but a model is also a useful analytical tool and in using it one begins to be able to move tentatively towards explanation and therefore prediction, for religious studies is not only an historical discipline.

J.H.
November 1982

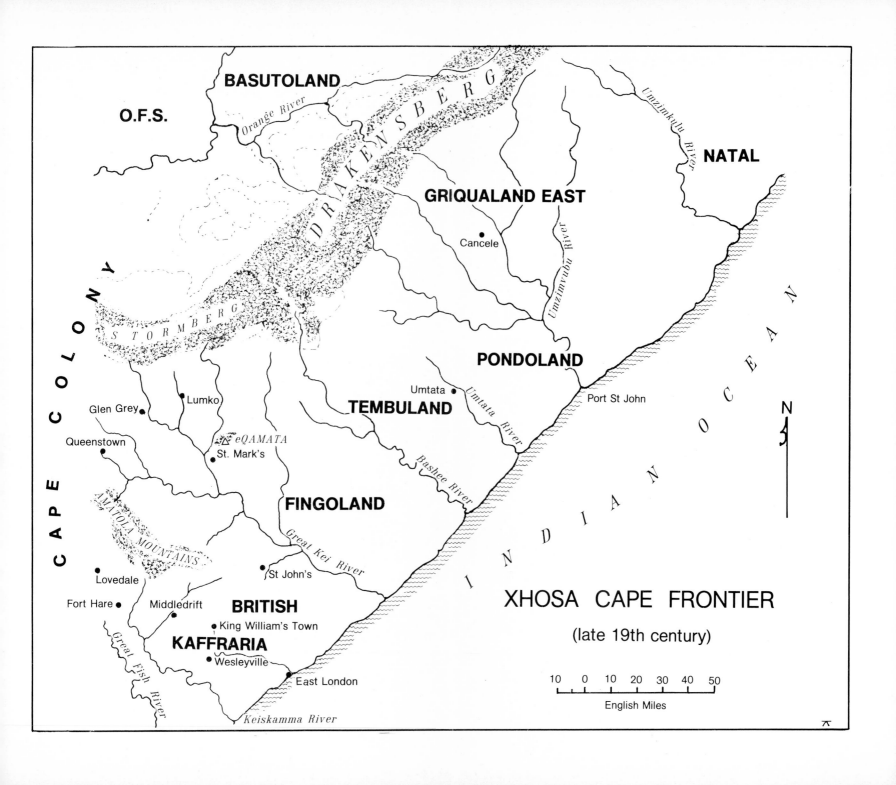

BASUTOLAND

O.F.S.

Orange River

DRAKENSBERG

Umzimkulu River

NATAL

GRIQUALAND EAST

Cancele

Umzimvubu River

C
A
P
E

C
O
L
O
N
Y

S T O R M B E R G

PONDOLAND

Lumko

Umtata

TEMBULAND

Umtata River

Port St John

Glen Grey

eQAMATA

St. Mark's

Queenstown

Bashee River

I
N
D
I
A
N

O
C
E
A
N

AMATOLA MOUNTAINS

FINGOLAND

Great Kei River

Lovedale

St John's

Fort Hare

Middledrift

BRITISH

King William's Town

Great Fish River

KAFFRARIA

Wesleyville

East London

Keiskamma River

XHOSA CAPE FRONTIER

(late 19th century)

N

10 0 10 20 30 40 50

English Miles

PART 1

1. INTRODUCTION

This historical study is an attempt to bring together what little is known about the myths of the Xhosa-speaking people and the origins and development of their traditional concepts of the supreme being. The lack of archaeological evidence and cultural-historical information makes the reconstruction of Xhosa religious history a difficult task. Even having resort to linguistic evidence, many of my findings must of necessity remain speculative and raise questions that cannot be settled on the available information.[1]

Nonetheless, I believe that this type of documentation provides a historical dimension which can deepen our understanding of religious and social change among the Xhosa, more especially the impact of Christianity in the last century and new religious developments in this. In addition, the resurgence of interest in traditional beliefs and customs, which is an integral part of the black cultural renaissance of today, calls for academic support.

In a pre-literate society like that of the Xhosa, the living tradition tends to be conservative but not static, having built into it the possibilities of change. Although it serves to preserve images of the past, it also incorporates images of the present and this gives it flexibility. As Mabona rightly observes, it 'is becoming increasingly appreciated, that African traditional religions were dynamic systems, continually adapting themselves, where necessary, to new developments'.[2] The problem is that custom is regarded as being sacrosanct and the change which does take place, albeit slowly, is generally denied. It is therefore only possible to dig under the surface to discover what might be learnt of the most likely course of religious change, in this case the traditional concepts of deity.

An attempt was made to collect oral information from contemporary authorities but this met with limited success. The radical religious and social changes wrought by Christianity and westernization from the beginning of the 19th century have resulted in a highly mixed cultural situation and many of the past traditions have been lost to posterity. As the new way of

3

life imposed itself upon the old, the wisdom of the aged no longer came to be revered and the ancient beliefs were either reinterpreted to conform to new beliefs and customs, or else were forgotten after the death of the custodians of the cultural and religious traditions.[3]

This study is largely based on the written records of early missionaries and travellers among the Xhosa. The presentation of this material suffers from the inevitable Eurocentric bias which regards Christianity as the religious norm and views the traditional beliefs and customs as being 'heathen and barbaric'.

However, much of this information was collected from Xhosa antiquaries and there is sufficient corroborating evidence to give the substance credence. Comparative documentation drawn from other indigenous societies in Southern Africa gives added support. The early Xhosa writers were also concerned with collecting their history and oral traditions, but a reading in of Christian content by these mission-educated converts is often detrimental to the historical value of their work. Even so, some of this information was clearly written down as narrated by the old people and is another valuable source.

In assessing the oral traditions as a whole, it must be remembered that they do not set out to be historically verifiable by the criteria of the modern scientific historian, and are open to many forms of distortion.[4] At the same time they were and are authoritative to the Xhosa and had and have no less impact for any lack of historical veracity. The indigenous people of Africa do not regard history as an end in itself; its value is symbolic. Therefore, in order to gain an insight into the blending of myth and history, which provides the framework for this study, it is first necessary to take into account the social and religious experience of the Xhosa.

NOTES AND REFERENCES

1. These sort of problems are fully dealt with in T. O. Ranger and I. N. Kimambo (eds.), *The Historical Study of African Religion* (Berkeley and Los Angeles, 1972).
2. M. A. Mabona, 'The Interaction and Development of different Religions

4

in the Eastern Cape in the late eighteenth and early nineteenth Centuries, with special reference to the first two Xhosa prophets'. (Essay, SOAS, University of London, 1973) p. 3.

3. For further discussion see E. B. Idowu, *African Traditional Religion: A Definition* (London, 1973) pp. 78–83.

4. For a discussion of the different forms of distortion common to Xhosa historiography see J. B. Peires, 'A History of the Xhosa *c.* 1700–1835' (M.A. thesis, Rhodes University, 1976) pp. 13–15, 123.

2. BACKGROUND TO XHOSA HISTORY AND SOCIETY: THEIR INTERACTION WITH KHOISAN

Of primary importance is the fact that the Xhosa were on the move over an extended period of time, coming into contact with people of other cultures with whom they intermarried. There has been considerable speculation as to where the parent body, the abeNguni, originally came from, by what routes they migrated south, and when this movement took place.[1] Westphal uses linguistic evidence to conclude that one important point of entry was across the lower Zambezi; but admits that this must still be corroborated by historical studies.[2] Archaeological evidence has been used to suggest that the ancestral Nguni were settled in Natal by the 11th century, but the connections are tenuous.[3]

In an attempt to dispel the myth-making, Wilson analyses the evidence from three sources: the written records of survivors from shipwrecks on the south-east coastline, oral traditions and archaeological investigations. She argues convincingly that the main movement of Nguni peoples occurred before the period covered by Xhosa genealogies, i.e. *circa* 1300, and that it may well have been centuries before that.[4] What is of greater significance, though, is that the evidence seems to indicate that Nguni-speakers were settled south of the Mthatha River before the end of the 16th century.[5] According to tradition, the Xhosa, Pondomise and Thembu lived in the foothills of the Drakensberg before coming to the coast. They are then thought to have moved gradually westward over a period of three hundred years, from about 1550 to 1850.[6] This was done in a fragmentary manner and Peires rightly describes it as expansion rather than migration. He also makes the important observation that all persons or groups who accepted the rule of the royal chiefdom (Tshawe) were incorporated as Xhosa, 'being given the full rights of any other Xhosa'.[7] Hence the heterogenous nature of the Xhosa nation.

Reports by Portuguese survivors of shipwrecks along the

south-east coast during the 16th and 17th centuries show that the Nguni people herded cattle, hunted game, cultivated sorghum, 'lived in beehive shaped huts in scattered homesteads and were ruled over by chiefs whom they called *inkosi*'.[8] One of the main reasons for Xhosa expansion was the hiving off of the sons of reigning chiefs to found new chiefdoms of their own, so relieving the political pressure at the centre of the kingdom.[9] Movement was also precipitated by the need to find new hunting grounds and fresh pastures.[10] It has been suggested that the heavily wooded nature of the area contributed towards the relatively slow rate of progress because the forest had to be burnt to provide grazing prior to occupation.[11]

Xhosa expansion met with little resistance until it reached the Kei River. The land east of the Kei was originally occupied by roving bands of 'hunter-gatherers' generally known as San or Bushmen.[12] As the Xhosa penetrated further the San were driven from their hunting grounds to seek refuge in the mountain strongholds of the Drakensberg. But some established a symbiotic relationship with the Xhosa and continued to occupy the same territory. Intermarriage took place on a limited scale. Xhosa tradition records that Sikhomo was the first chief to marry a San woman, but that she ran away to her home on the Orange River after the birth of a son.[13] This was probably in the 17th century.

West of the Kei lived scattered groups of semi-nomadic 'hunter-herders' known as Khoi (Khoikhoi) or Hottentots. Available linguistic and archaeological evidence indicates that they had occupied this area for many centuries.[14] There was some active resistance among the Khoi to the Xhosa advance; but on the whole friendly relations were established between them and they lived side by side for many years.[15] Although quite a number of Xhosa refugees were absorbed into Khoi chiefdoms, the general trend was for the Khoi gradually to become incorporated into Xhosa society in a patron-client relationship.[16] While the link was initially established through trade, extensive intermarriage, led by the respective royal lineages, opened the way for cultural diffusion.[17] Peires notes that, 'it is certain that a Khoi who entered Xhosa society did so on terms of distinct inferiority, but since this inferiority was

7

expressed in economic terms and not in social or racial ones, it passed within the course of a generation'.[18] Mixed Khoi and Xhosa communities are recorded by European travellers in Ciskei and Transkei from the 18th century on.

The 'clicks' or implosive consonants in the Xhosa language indicate the extent of Khoisan influence on Xhosa culture.[19] Linguistic evidence suggests that interaction could have taken place over as long a period as four centuries,[20] and it could well have been longer. One sixth of all Xhosa words contain clicks, but of the 2 400 click words in Xhosa only 375 have cognates in Zulu.[21] Thus the indications are that the Xhosa acquired the majority of the click words in their language after they separated from the parent Nguni body. This is significant for the historical study of the religious development of the Xhosa. Firstly, the linguistic evidence shows that cultural interaction with the Khoisan took place while the Xhosa and Zulu still belonged to a common stock, and can be dated from before 1300.[22] Secondly, it shows that the Xhosa incorporated a large number of religious terms from the Khoisan, and that those that are not present in the Zulu language must have been acquired during the period of Xhosa expansion through Transkei and Ciskei.

Harinck suggests that the inferior social status of the Khoi was balanced by a high religious status, and reasons that this was attributed to them by the Xhosa in the belief that as the original occupants of the land they had a special ability to protect it.[23] Peires disputes this hypothesis for lack of supporting evidence; but he does not say by whose authority or on what evidence he bases his statement that while most rainmakers around 1805 were Khoi, 'they were later superseded by the Mfengu, who had even less title to the land than the Xhosa'.[24] In the 1830s, Backhouse makes a sweeping generalization that 'almost the whole of the Caffre doctors are of the Fingo nation'.[25] While Mfengu diviners certainly seem to have enjoyed popularity among the Xhosa of Ciskei after 1835, there is no proof that they entirely eclipsed their Xhosa colleagues. Hirst notes that in traditional Xhosa society the profession of diviner was open to anyone who had experienced the 'call of the ancestors', and this included the Khoi and the Mfengu as well as the Xhosa proper.[26] In some parts the San were renowned as rainmakers, too,[27] and even the first missionaries were cast in this role.[28]

Hirst also makes the point that the *materia medica* of the Xhosa *amagqirha* depended on locally occurring trees, plants and herbs. Certain of these plants occur only in specific ecological settings. Migration into new territory would necessitate learning about the new environment from the already established inhabitants, no matter that they might have been conquered. Modern diviners in Ciskei can distinguish several medicinal plants that the Xhosa incorporated from the Khoi and San at some stage in the past, and this explains why the Xhosa at first made use of these people as rainmakers. The Khoisan are said to have obtained knowledge of medicinal plants, as the Xhosa ancestors did, by observing the eating habits of wild animals especially the mammalian species.[29]

The extent of Khoisan influence on Xhosa belief and customs is debatable, and awaits further analysis, but there is no doubt that interaction took place at a deep cultural level.[30] There is evidence to show that the mutual influences of their myths of life and death influenced both Khoi and Xhosa ritual, and that the more developed Khoisan notions of the supreme being brought about changes in the Xhosa world-view and religious practice. It is on these aspects that I shall be focusing.

From the evidence it is clear that warfare, trade and intermarriage between San, Khoi and Xhosa would result in time in the formation of social relationships, as kinsmen if nothing else; and that one of the results of this interaction would be cultural diffusion.[31] However, although one can come to the general conclusion that the incorporation of large numbers of Khoisan individuals into Xhosa society provided the opportunity for the Xhosa to incorporate new ideas from the Khoisan, of specific interest for the study of religious change is what influences were at work in determining the selection and acceptance of particular elements from the Khoisan tradition by the Xhosa.

With the distance in time and the scanty evidence available there can be no certainty as to the effects of geographical movement and cultural diffusion on the Xhosa prior to 1800; but I suggest that their socio-cultural experience had been sufficiently disturbed to create a need for new modes of explanation and control to cope with new situations, more especially the strange ecological environment and the foreign way of life of the Khoisan, and that the process of change that I will be tracing will show how these needs were fulfilled by assimilating new religious ideas and practices from the Khoisan. This can be seen to correspond with what Cumpsty refers to as the 'Search Stage' in his 'Model of Change in Socio-Cultural Disturbance'.[32]

In the 'Search Stage' the pace of change is not great enough to create insecurity: social cohesion has not yet been threatened and the authority of the tradition remains intact; but there is nonetheless a need to fill an almost unconscious symbol vacuum and to find a new source of power with which to cope with new situations. Cumpsty argues that there would then 'be a search for elements from the incoming tradition with which to understand its own gradually changing sense of reality and at the same time a move to give new meaning to suitable elements of its own tradition'.[33] Among the Xhosa the search led to accommodation with the incoming tradition of the Khoisan and, as Hirst rightly observes, the accretion of new elements would be 'at precisely those points where the conventional theory fails to satisfactorily interpret and translate the inexplicable in every day social life and human experience'.[34]

I see the religious changes that took place among the Xhosa during the period under discussion as being part of an ongoing process, supporting the view already expressed that the traditional Xhosa religious system was dynamic and was adaptable to new developments, the needs of specific situations determining the pattern of change. Lack of evidence about earlier Xhosa history has unfortunately limited the scope of this study. It is not possible to trace the general process of change from an earlier time, nor is it possible to assess how much the religious changes analysed below are partly a response to contemporary socio-economic and political change, such as the growth of long-distance trade or change in the role of chieftainship; but it is evident that the increasing contact with the white man at the beginning of the 19th century heightened the needs of the Xhosa in a context of increasing socio-cultural disturbance.

It is my contention that as a result of the incorporation of Khoisan elements into the Xhosa religious tradition, the way was prepared for the interpretation of Christianity within this tradition. This is well illustrated by the teaching of the Xhosa prophet Ntsikana between the time of his conversion around 1815 and his death in 1821. He met with far greater success than the early missionaries, who attempted to graft Christianity directly onto Xhosa culture. His theology is enshrined in his four hymns and they represent a truly African expression of Christianity.[35] This supports the view that the religious transformations brought about by Christianity were part of an ongoing process of religious change among the Xhosa, albeit intensified and at a greater pace; and that Christian doctrine only became a meaningful part of Xhosa culture when it began to meet their existential and interpretative needs.

NOTES AND REFERENCES

1. E.g. G. M. Theal, *Ethnography and Conditions of South Africa before 1505* (London, 1910) p. 193. I am greatly indebted to Manton Hirst who marshalled together much of the evidence in the following discussion in a commendable attempt to distinguish fact from fiction.
2. E. O. J. Westphal, 'The Linguistic Prehistory of Southern Africa: Bush, Kwadi, Hottentot, and Bantu Linguistic Relationships', *Africa* 33 (3): p. 264, 1963.
3. R. R. Inskeep, *The Peopling of Southern Africa* (Cape Town, 1978) p. 145.
4. M. Wilson, 'The Early History of the Transkei and Ciskei', *African Studies* 18 (4): p. 178, 1959.
5. Wilson (1959), pp. 167–74; M. Wilson and L. Thompson, *The Oxford History of South Africa* I (Oxford, 1969) pp. 78–87. cf. Inskeep (1978), p. 153.
6. Wilson (1959), p. 176. M. Cronin's excavation of an early Iron Age site on the Transkeian coast has been dated 7th and 8th Century AD, but there is no certainty as to whether the occupants were Khoi or Bantu-speaking, *East London Daily Dispatch*, 3 August 1978.
7. J. B. Peires, *The House of Phalo: A History of the Xhosa People in the Days of their Independence* (Johannesburg, 1981) p. 19.
8. D. Birmingham and S. Marks, 'Southern Africa' in *Cambridge History of Africa* III, edited by R. Oliver (Cambridge, 1977) p. 616.
9. Peires (1981), pp. 20–21.
10. W. K. Kaye, MS 172c, Grey Collection, South African Library.
11. Birmingham and Marks (1977), p. 616.
12. For a discussion on the problems of terminology see R. Elphick, *Kraal and Castle. Khoikhoi and the Founding of White South Africa* (New Haven and

11

London, 1977) pp. xxi–xxii; and Westphal (1963). The term 'hunter-gatherer' denotes people who lived by what they could hunt and gather from their environment. The 'hunter-herders' are those who herded cattle as well as hunted.

13. W. B. Rubusana, *Zemk'iinkomo Magwalandini* (abridged ed., Lovedale, 1966) p. 80.
14. Cf. R. M. Derricourt, *Prehistoric Man in the Ciskei and Transkei* (Cape Town and Johannesburg, 1977); Elphick (1977), ch. 1; G. Harinck, 'Interaction between Xhosa and Khoi: Emphasis on the period 1620–1750' in *African Societies in Southern Africa*, edited by L. Thompson (London, 1969) pp. 145–69.
15. For a general discussion on the relations of the Xhosa with Khoi and San see Wilson and Thompson (1969), pp. 102–7.
16. Harinck (1969).
17. Mabona (1973) provides evidence that Khoi wives 'rated a special favour with the Xhosa', p. 1.
18. Peires (1981), p. 23.
19. According to Westphal (1963), Proto-Khoi did not contain clicks so that they are probably of Central Bushman origin.
20. R. Derricourt, 'Settlement in the Transkei and Ciskei before the Mfecane' in *Beyond the Cape Frontier. Studies in the History of the Transkei and Ciskei*, edited by C. Saunders and R. Derricourt (London, 1974) p. 52.
21. W. Bourquin, 'Click Words which Xhosa, Zulu and Sotho have in common', *African Studies* 10–11: pp. 59–81, 1951–52; L. W. Lanham, 'The proliferation and extension of Bantu phonemic systems influenced by Bushman and Hottentot,' *Proceedings of the Ninth International Congress of Linguistics*, Cambridge, Mass. 1962 (The Hague, 1964) pp. 382–91.
22. Wilson (1959), p. 177, also notes that the association between Xhosa and Khoisan must pre-date the period covered by Xhosa genealogies, since they contain names with clicks.
23. Harinck (1969), pp. 151–3. See also L. F. Maingard, 'The Linguistic Approach to South African Prehistory and Ethnology', *South African Journal of Science* XXXI: pp. 132–4, 1934.
24. Peires (1981), p. 65.
25. J. Backhouse, *A Narrative of a Visit to the Mauritius and South Africa* (London, 1844) p. 231.
26. This discussion is largely based on the evidence and argument provided by M. Hirst, personal communication, 8 October 1981.
27. Wilson (1959), p. 177, notes that the Mpondomise depended upon the San as rainmakers. See also F. Brownlee, *The Transkeian Native Territories: Historical Records* (Lovedale, 1923) p. 123; Peires (1981), p. 24.
28. Cf. W. Shaw, *The Story of My Mission in South-Eastern Africa* (London, 1860) pp. 460–6; H. A. Reyburn, 'The Missionary as Rainmaker', *The Critic* 1 (8): pp. 146–53, 1933.
29. M. Hirst, personal communication, 8 October 1981.
30. Mabona (1973), p. 2.

31. M. Hirst, personal communication, 8 October 1981. I am also indebted to Fr. D. J. Dargie for his contribution to this discussion: personal communication, 26 February 1982.
32. J. S. Cumpsty, 'A Model of Religious Change in Socio-Cultural Disturbance', *Religion in Southern Africa* 1 (2): p. 66, July 1980.
33. Ibid.
34. M. Hirst, personal communication, 8 October 1981.
35. J. Hodgson, *Ntsikana's 'Great Hymn'. A Xhosa Expression of Christianity in the Early 19th Century Eastern Cape* (Communications No. 4, Centre for African Studies, University of Cape Town, 1980).

PART II

3. COSMOGONIC MYTHS

The Monistic World-View of the Xhosa

The traditional religion of the Xhosa falls together with other African traditional religions into that type which Cumpsty has classified as 'Nature Religion'.[1] An essential feature of this type is that no radical gap exists between the gods and the realm of nature including man. The cosmogonic myths of the Xhosa are typical in lacking the critical factor of *creatio ex nihilo*. Without a radical gap between nature and the 'gods' religion cannot be a separate category of thought or experience. It is all-pervasive and therefore participates with the 'divine' in one monistic experience. It is characterized by a cosmic oneness: 'No distinction can be made between sacred and secular, between natural and supernatural, for Nature, Man and the Unseen are inseparably involved in one another in a total community'.[2]

As with the ancient Semitic religions, Xhosa and other African traditional religions have what Cumpsty describes as a weak belief structure in the sense that there is little of it, there is little pressure for logical coherence, and a knowledge of it is not the significant criterion for belonging to the group. There is rather a seeking and feeling after an underlying order of things through myth and ritual without demanding exactitude or finality. All the necessary knowledge has been given in the beginning in myth and this has been handed down in the oral tradition. The Golden Age is always in the past, and conservatism is highly valued.[3] Wisdom is a knowledge of the tradition and custom related to the past.

In the mythopoeic world-view of the traditional African, the mythological past is constantly recoverable in ritual because time is eternal. It has no real beginning, and because of that it has no real destiny.[4] All is one and is pervaded by divinity. Where everything is seen as being fulfilled in the eternal cycle of existence, the individual does not find, his meaning, as Fawcett says, by being absorbed into the divine,[5] for he is already one with the divine, but by maintaining harmonious relationships within his cosmos.

Myths of Origin : the Emergence from a Hole or Cave

Like most African myths, the Xhosa myths are primarily concerned with the origin of man and the world around him. They are not creation stories. Rather, they are part of the socialization process, a kind of 'just so' story told to children by their elders to satisfy their curiosity. The myths describe how the first man and woman, together with their animals, appeared on earth from a previous existence. The so-called 'Creator', perhaps better, originator, is conceived as enabling them to emerge. Common to the different versions of the Xhosa cosmogonic myth is the idea that men and animals formerly existed in caverns in the bowels of the earth. At length they are said to have come forth out of this underworld through an immense hole, the opening of which was either in a cavern or else in a marsh overgrown with reeds.[6] Similar ideas are reported for other peoples in Southern Africa.[7] Xhosa oral traditions refer to their place of origin as *Eluhlangeni* or *umhlanga*. Today, this is widely understood as being 'the place of reeds';[8] but it is also the locative form of *uhlanga*, and this was translated by Nicholson (1858) as 'cave' for the Xhosa and Thembu, and 'reed' only for the Zulu-speaking people.[9]

According to Mabona, the *abantu bomlambo* or mythical river people are those who remained in the place of origin when mankind came out of the hole. They are therefore reputed to be very wise and powerful, and are associated with the ancestors.[10]

Alberti recorded one of the earliest versions of the Xhosa myth of origin in 1807, claiming to impart it 'in the manner in which it is related by the Kaffirs themselves':

> In the land in which the sun rises, there was a cavern from which the first Kaffirs, and in fact All peoples, as also the stock of every kind of animal came forth. At the same time, the sun and moon came into being, to shed their light, and trees, grass and other plants to provide food for man and cattle.[11]

An even earlier version, recorded by the crew of the *Stavenisse* in 1689, explains the origin of the social life of the Xhosa. It relates that 'they deduce their origin from a certain man and woman who grew up together out of the earth, and who taught them to cultivate the ground, to sow corn, milk cows, and brew beer'.[12]

The idea of man and beast emerging from some sort of subterranean hole or cavern is widespread in Central and West Africa, as well as in other southern parts, although the myths only sometimes mention the 'Creator's' role in bringing them forth. Indentations on surrounding rocks, whether they be the fossilized tracks of prehistoric animals or the work of wind and water, are popularly believed to be the footprints of the first men and their animals.[13] Generally the place is reputed to be either in the north or in the east, depending on the direction from which the people originally migrated, or perhaps linked for some with the rising sun. Xhosa sources are unanimous in speaking of 'a cavern in the east', which is called *uhlanga*. This cosmological association with the east has a ritual significance because traditionally the entrance to the main hut in the homestead faced east, and the chiefs were also buried facing east.[14] These practices continue to this day, with graves being sited on an eastern axis; but the original significance has been forgotten and it is purely a matter of custom.[15]

Lichtenstein, writing sometime between 1803 and 1806, reported that a current belief among the Xhosa was that cows and oxen might still be procured from the cavern in great abundance, if only the entrance could again be found and a suitable bait silently laid by which the cattle might be enticed out, and then captured.[16] A few years later, Campbell noted that because of the tradition that the oxen came out of a hole in Tambookie (Thembu) country, the Xhosa paid an annual tribute to them, 'in gratitude for this blessing'.[17]

A more detailed version of the myth linking *uhlanga* with the cavern in the east was recorded from the oral tradition by Ayliff in 1846. In this account the cattle are said to have emerged first, followed by mankind, and then various beasts, birds etc., in consecutive order. There is also a description of how, after many unsuccessful attempts, mankind eventually domesticated the cattle. They were lured to the cavern entrance by the smell of blood, and, as they stood round the spot bellowing, were surrounded and taken.[18] This is another typical 'just so' story illustrating the socialization process in a peasant society.

Myths explaining the Origin of Different Races

Tiyo Soga set down a similar version but with significant additional details which provide an explanation for racial differences; but the earliest such myth was recounted by Robert Balfour Noyi in his 'Ama-Xhosa history' in 1848. According to Noyi, Xhosa 'traditionists' were as yet only concerned with the origin and character of three races: Hottentot, Xhosa and Bushman. Oral tradition relates:

> A certain man had three sons, whose names were Ibranana, Xosa, and Twa. Ibranana was a keeper of cattle, sheep, and goats, as was also Xosa, while poor Twa was satisfied with his honey bird and his game in the desert. Ibranana (the ancestor of the Hottentots) was not a tall man, and his complexion was sallow. Twa (the ancestor of the Bushman) was shorter still and more slender, and also of a sallow complexion, but a shade lighter. And Xosa was a tall, muscular man, and dark coloured.[19]

Noyi ends by saying that these descriptions obviously referred to the progenitors of the different races. Tiyo Soga collected his material about twenty years later.[20] According to his informants, *uhlanga* was a place with three large holes. The black man emerged from one, the white man from another, and the lower animals from the third: man coming before the animals.[21] So it was that the details were changed to incorporate the advent of the white man into Xhosa cosmogony.

J. H. Soga gives what he says is a modern version of the creation myth, told at the expense of the Hottentot:

> At the creation . . . the white man, on whom was expended a good deal of time, was turned out a finished article, so also with the black man: but the end of the week intervened before the Hottentot was completed, and the work was suspended until the following week, when it was found that the clay had hardened. Nothing further could be done, and

the Hottentot was left unfinished, as he is to-day, – an incomplete man.[22]

Soga also provides further information about man's strategem to domesticate horses and other animals besides cattle. Initially animals are said to have evaded capture by only grazing in the vicinity of their hole and disappearing into it as soon as men appeared. In the end they were drawn from their refuge by the scent of a putrid dog dragged along the ground. Attracted by curious fear, they became maddened with excitement and as they rushed past snorting and bellowing, the watching men were able to cut off their retreat and trap them in ready prepared enclosures. Soga's story of the 'creation' then goes on to explain how the different racial groups acquired their lot in life, showing how the new and strange is made explicable and meaningful in the context of a living myth.

> The oldest son of the father of all was a Hottentot; the second a Kafir; the third a white man. No creature could have been more happily situated than the Hottentot. He revelled in the abundance of his father's riches and luxuries. At length, by reason of the abundance in which he moved, he grew careless, indolent, and utterly regardless. His great amusement was to follow the honey-bird from day to day in search of bee-hives. One day he went out as usual, and and never returned to his father, leaving everything behind him. That is the reason given why the Hottentots are such an improvident people.
>
> The second son, the Kafir, took a special liking to cattle, and the herding of them. Cattle ultimately became his inheritance; and when he came of age, he left his father, and set up for himself. That is why the Kafirs are to this day so fond of cattle. The other thing, received from his father, to retain for ever as his inalienable property, was Kafir corn, for which he has a special liking.
>
> While the oldest son, the Hottentot, was pursuing his wandering chase after the honey-bird, and the second son, the Kafir, was following his flocks in the fields, the youngest son, the white man, was always at home with the old man, his father. As the youngest, he was a great favourite. He was constantly in his father's company, waiting upon him, and

hearing his wise talk. In this way he became a precocious child. His father poured into his *'soft head'* all the treasures of wisdom and knowledge. He told him everything; showed him how to do all things; and thus the white man was far in advance of the other races.' [23]

There is a remarkable correspondence between this legend and the story told to Thomas Bain by 'a very intelligent old Kafir', at much the same time.[24] An account 'Of the Creation of People' by William Kekale Kaye, 'a native interpreter', is un-dated but was probably written during the same period. Here there is an ingenious attempt to bring Xhosa myth into line with biblical teaching, the second and third chapters of Genesis being presented in a traditional idiom. God becomes the Chief, Satan the cook. Man is created from earth and cloud, while woman is made from a mixture of man's short rib, cloud and moon (the inclusion of moon explaining why women have a regular 'monthly illness'). They all live in round grass huts and man tends cattle. The story of the Xhosa Garden of Eden fol-lows the biblical model, the myth of 'paradise lost' providing a new explanation for the origin of suffering, illness and death.[25]

This must have found echoes for a people whose traditional belief system is explanatory, denying the idea of chance and being preoccupied with the causes of misfortune. What is even more radical, however, is the introduction of the notion of *creatio ex nihilo*, permitted by the development in the sense of the divine as a transcendent being.

The Reed Myths of Origin

Kropf distinguishes between the use of *uhlanga* in Xhosa as the place or hole from which all living beings came forth originally, and an old stalk of Kaffircorn or maize.[26] The two different meanings can be linked with the two main forms of the myth about the origin of man found among the Nguni, the one which has already been discussed concerning the cavern in the east, and the other relating to a reed or reed bed. The Zulu meaning of *uhlanga* is 'a stalk of grain', 'a reed', 'reedy place' or 'original stem or stock of the tribe or people';[27] and these correspond with the popular Zulu cosmogonic narratives. One strand of the myth says that deity 'created the first human being by splitting a reed, from which came a man and two women, who were the progenitors of the human race'. [28] The other form, with variants, describes mankind emerging with his animals from a bed of reeds, coming out of water, by the sea, with the assistance of deity.[29] The earliest recorded version linking the Xhosa place of origin with reeds is Holden's in 1866, which suggests that this form of the myth is of Zulu derivation. This supposition is strengthened by Nicholson's evidence in 1858, that while *uhlanga* signified 'reed' for the Natal tribes, it was generally used as 'cave' among the Xhosa and Thembu. It is possible that the 'reed' myth was the original version shared by both branches of the abeNguni, but that among the Xhosa it was superseded by the 'cave' myth after they came into contact with the Khoisan. It could then have been reintroduced by the Mfengu, the Zulu refugees who settled among the Xhosa from the 1820s on. This argument is supported by Derricourt's observation that the word *umhlanga*, which has the same meaning as *uhlanga* in Zulu, is used in Xhosa for a wild grass and was probably introduced to them by the Mfengu.[30] Nowadays the 'reed' myth is the only version known in the Ciskei.

Khoisan Myths of Origin

The information about the Khoisan myths of origin is rather slender; but in 1779, Wikar noted that there was 'a general superstition' among a number of different Khoi clans on the west coast, that their cattle came out of a hole in a flat rock, and that the spoor of the cattle could be seen on the stone.[31] Stow reported that according to the myth of origin of the San tribes around the lower Gariep, their remote forefathers came out of a hole in the ground at the roots of an enormous tree which covered a wide extent of the country. Immediately afterwards all kinds of animals came swarming out after them in great numbers.[32] According to Mabona, both the Khoi and the San identify the first ancestor with the dawn-tree, 'which, being a cosmic phenomenon, is only metaphorically a tree and is therefore just "any tree".'[33] But the Khoi in fact identify

23

the first ancestor root as being that of the mimosa tree, *nqo-mab*.[34] It was their custom to pray in the bushes,[35] and this practice seems to have been taken up by the Xhosa.[36]

The link between cosmogony and the east is well documented among the Khoi. It is said to be the direction from which their 'grandfather *Tsui//Goab*' and their 'ancestor *Heitsi Eibib*' came, bringing with them plenty of cattle and sheep. The Pleiades, which feature in their religious ritual, are also associated with the east. The Khoi told Hahn that the east was their 'Fatherland', and that is why the doors of their huts faced east, their graves were all directed towards the east and the face of the deceased was always turned in that direction.[37] Again this could be the origin of the similar customs among the Xhosa, as mentioned previously.[38] However, the Xhosa do not appear to have followed the Khoi custom of leaving their huts at dawn to go and pray facing towards the east.[39]

There is another body of cosmogonic myths among the Khoi that associates the hole from which the first man and woman came forth as being in the sky. It was recorded by Kolb in 1731 as follows:

> The Hottentots say, their First Parents came into their Country through a Window or Door-Passage (the Word for both in the Hottentot-Tongue being the same), that the Name of the Man was Nôh, and of the Woman Hingnôh: that they were sent into their Country by God himself, whom they call Tiquoa: And that they taught their Descendants to keep Cattle, and to do a great many other things.[40]

Grevenbroek's (1695) version corresponds and then goes on to give the origin of certain social practices. His informants told him that the progenitors of their race taught mankind and his ancestors 'to marry wives and rear children, to practice polygamy, peace and concord, to hurt no one, to give to each his own, together with other similar precepts'.[41] Some Khoi maintained that the first people had descended from the sky in 'a great basket'.[42] The Zulu are reported as having a similar tradition.[43] Grevenbroek also recorded a Xhosa myth which ascribed their origin 'to a man and his wife who in remote times descended through a window on to the earth';[44] but as this is the only such version for the Xhosa it would seem to be of Khoi derivation.

Other Traditions

Apart from dealing with the origin of man, most indigenous myths in Africa concentrate on the origin of important social and ritual institutions. They explain 'the basic conditions of human life as the people now find it'.[45] Typical of such myths among the Xhosa are those relating 'the origin of the mantis', 'a person on the moon' and the 'discovery' of pumpkin and kaffircorn.[46] The early written records of the tradition agree that according to Xhosa myth, 'the first parents' were responsible for teaching the people about 'agriculture and the storing of grains and berries, the milking of cattle, the brewing of beer and the making of bread'.[47]

The modern usage of *uhlanga* in Xhosa as a nation, race or people was a logical progression from its primary meaning as 'the original stem or stock'. The development of this derivation can be traced in the oral tradition recorded by Steedman in 1835, in which the first Great Chief was said to have come out of a cave to the east called *uDaliwe*.[48] Derricourt gives the meaning of *uDaliwe* as 'being created',[49] thus linking the first ancestor with the cosmogonic myth. Fifty years later William Gqoba went a step further. He recounts an oral tradition that *Untu* was the first chief from whom all others are descended, and that he was the father of Zulu and Xhosa. Gqoba continues:

> When we ask who the father of Untu was, we are answered that he was the son of *Eluhlangeni* or *wo-Hlanga*, which means he sprang from the nation. Other tribes use the verb *ukuhlaluka* about Untu, and say he appeared from the race, and brought with him all their laws, habits, customs, etc.[50]

According to Kropf, *umntu* means a human being, the plural of which is *abantu*, men, people; while *ubuntu* means human nature, humanity, manhood.[51] The Xhosa say that *uNtu* is the progenitor of the *abantu*.[52]

25

Xhosa Myth and History

We have seen that *uhlanga* is synonymous with 'the source'; but the Xhosa no longer use it in this way and Derricourt presumes that missionary activity was responsible for the loss of its mythological connection.[53] Nevertheless, the cosmogonic myth has had a profound influence on Xhosa history which is not generally realised.[54]

Traditionally the Xhosa had only a shadowy concept of the supreme being, related to whom there was neither a clearly defined belief nor system of worship. It was the ancestors, i.e. the spirits of the dead members of the lineage, who were the focus of religious activity in their daily lives. The ancestors were thought to be present in and around the homestead, but they were also believed to live in a spirit-world, either below ground or below water, and this can be related to the myth of origin.

In the early 19th century, the coming of the white man put increasing pressure on Xhosa society. Resistance took the form of cattle-stealing and armed conflict. But it became increasingly clear to the Xhosa that the traditional forms of resistance were ineffective against the British might. Consequently, they sought to tap new sources of power through the 'prophets' who emerged to meet the need of a socio-cultural disturbance that was unprecedented in their history. Nxele (Makhanda) in 1819 was followed by Mlanjeni in 1850, and Nongqawuse and Mhlakaza in 1856. The expectation was of a mass resurrection of the ancestors, who would help drive the white man into the sea; and a return to a Golden Age of prosperity and eternal peace. The corporate resurrection can be seen as a millenarian concept assimilated from Christianity to revitalize the tradition; but, as certain significant features show, it is grounded in the ancient cosmological thought-patterns and therefore acquired plausibility.

For example, Nxele said that he had been sent by *Uhlanga*, the Great Spirit, to avenge his people's wrongs and that the dead would rise from their graves out of the sea to assist them; while Nongqawuse's meetings with messengers from the dead took place at a swampy pool, and she revealed that the ancestral spirits in the bowels of the earth would arise with abundant cattle out of pools all over the country. As the great day approached there were reported sightings of past heroes rising from the sea, and rushing through the air in battle array before disappearing again beneath the waves. The horns of cattle were also said to have been seen peeping from beneath rushes which grew around Nongqawuse's pool, and the knocking of horns and bellowing were supposedly heard as the cattle waited impatiently in a subterranean cave to come forth.[55]

The ritual propitiation of the ancestors by slaughtering cattle conformed with traditional belief and practice, except that with each successive 'prophet' it increased in scale. By the mid-1850s pressure on Xhosa society had become so severe that the appeal to the supernatural succeeded in transcending the fragmented political units, and 'the believers' united in performing a 'national sacrifice' that would propitiate the founding fathers of them all. It seems unlikely that there would have been such a wholesale destruction of animals and crops unless the Xhosa factions had shared a common mythological basis to their expectations.

Incidently, it was only after the failure of this movement had led to the disintegration of Xhosa society that missionary influence was seriously effective.

It seems clear that, under the influence of both the European disturbing presence and Christian ideas following upon a culturally fluid period in their own history, the traditional Xhosa cosmogonic myth became more concerned with a coming-to-be, which is nearer to the Christian understanding of creation, and ceased to reflect so strongly a time past at another level of existence. Yet it is clear that for Nxele the return of the dead was not simply resurrection from the grave but a coming again by the same route which the first ancestors of man had taken. And for Nongqawuse, the first signs of their coming was that of the accompanying herds; and that the cattle killing is not just an irrational act of appeasement of angry ancestors, but a sending back the cattle from whence they came in the assurance that they would come again bringing the ancestors with them. The timeless cyclical sense of the cosmos was clearly still present in spite of the pressures toward a more transcendent sense of deity, and its corollary, a beginning in time.

1. Cumpsty (1980), p. 60.
2. J. V. Taylor, *The Primal Vision. Christian Presence amid African Religion* (London, 1963) p. 64.
3. M. Wilson, *Religion and the Transformation of Society: A Study in Social Change in Africa* (Cambridge, 1971) p. 8.
4. J. S. Mbiti is widely quoted as saying that 'according to traditional concepts, time is a two-dimensional phenomenon, with a long *past*, a *present* and virtually *no future*. The linear concept of time in western thought, with an indefinite past, present and infinite future is practically foreign in African thinking': *African Religions and Philosophy* (London, 1969) p. 17.
5. T. Fawcett, *The Symbolic Language of Religion* (London, 1970) p. 214.
6. G. M. Theal (1910), p. 231. See also J. McKay, *The Origin of the Xhosa and others* (Cape Town, 1911) p. 52.
7. E.g. J. Campbell, *Travels in South Africa*, 1813 (London, 1815) p. 192; E. Casalis, *The Basutos* (London, 1861) pp. 240–1; W. C. Willoughby, *Nature – Worship and Taboo* (Hartford, 1932) p. 77; W. D. Hammond-Tooke (ed.), *The Bantu-Speaking Peoples of Southern Africa* (2nd ed., London, 1974) pp. 319–20.
8. H. M. Ndawo, *Uhambo luka Gqoboka* (Lovedale, n.d.) ch. 1; G. Nkonki, 'The Traditional Prose Literature of the Ngqika' (unpublished M.A. Thesis, Unisa, 1968) pp. 30–1.
9. B. Nicholson in J. Maclean (compiler), *A Compendium of Kaffir Laws and Customs* (Mount Coke, 1858) p. 170.
10. Mabona (1973), n. 24.
11. L. Alberti, *Alberti's Account of the Tribal Life and Customs of the Xhosa in 1807* (Cape Town, 1968) p. 13.
12. D. Moodie, *The Record: or a series of Official Papers relative to the Condition and Treatment of the Native Tribes of South Africa* (1840; reprint ed., Amsterdam and Cape Town, 1960) p. 431.
13. E.g. 'A Native Lad', 'A Native Legend of the Origin of Men and Animals,' *The Christian Express* XXXIII (395): pp. 122–3, 1 August 1903; J. Campbell, *Travels in South Africa . . . being a Narrative of a Second Journey, 1820* I (London, 1822) pp. 303, 306; R. Dart, 'Rock Engravings', *S. A. Journal of Science* XXVII: pp. 475–86, 1931; J. S. Mbiti, *Concepts of God in Africa* (London, 1970) pp. 151–2; R. Moffat, *Missionary Labours and Scenes in Southern Africa* (London, 1842) p. 69; J. Mpotokwane, 'Native Folklore', MS 1228, Cory Library, Rhodes University, p. 18; G. W. Stow, *The Native Races of South Africa* (London, 1905) pp. 261, 432–3; Willoughby (1932), pp. 65–75. H. J. Wikar reports a similar myth among the Hottentots in 1779, *The Journal of Hendrik Jacob Wikar* (1779) edited by E. Mossop (Cape Town, 1935) pp. 95–6; and Stow, for the Bushmen (1905), pp. 3, 130.
14. J. G. Grevenbroek, 'An Elegant and Accurate account of the African Race living round the Cape of Good Hope commonly called Hottentots (1695)

in *The Early Cape Hottentots*, edited by I. Schapera (Cape Town, 1933) p. 259; Stow (1905), p. 545.

15. Interview with M. Hirst, Kaffrarian Museum, King William's Town, 26 May 1981. See also H. Kuckertz, 'A symbol that interprets the World. Ancestor cult and ceremonially drinking beer in Mthwa society' (unpublished paper, Lumko, January 1981). Kuckertz's findings in Mpondoland are that the entrance to the hut faces north-east with the entrance to the cattle-byre almost opposite. Because the men always sit to the left of the entrance of the byre when ritually drinking beer, they look towards the east, facing in the same direction as the grave of the 'owner' who is buried beyond the byre.

16. H. Lichtenstein, *Travels in Southern Africa in the Years, 1803, 1804, 1805 and 1806* I (first published 1812–1815; Cape Town, V.R.S. 10, 1928) p. 314.

17. Campbell (1815), p. 368.

18. J. Ayliff, *A Vocabulary of the Kafir Language* (London, 1846) pp. v–vi.

19. R. B. Noyi, 'Ama-Xosa History', Appendix II in J. K. Bokwe, *Ntsikana: The Story of an African Convert* (2nd ed., Lovedale, 1914) p. 37 (translated by Rev. J. Bennie and first published in the *Glasgow Missionary Record*, 1848). For a comparable myth in South West Africa see H. Beiderbecke, 'Some Religious Ideas and Customs of the Ovaherero', *S. A. Folk-Lore Journal* II (part 5): pp. 93–7, Sept. 1880.

20. Tiyo Soga quoted in J. A. Chalmers, *Tiyo Soga: A Page of South African Mission Work* (Edinburgh and London, 1877) pp. 354–5. cf. the 'Creation Myth' of the Bayeye: Edwards, 'Tradition of the Bayeye', *S.A. Folk-Lore Journal* II (part 2): pp. 34–7, March 1880.

21. W. Schmidt's findings among Zulu and Xhosa traditional tales are that black and white had a common origin from one *uhlanga:* W. Wanger, 'The Zulu Notion of God according to the traditional Zulu God-names', *Anthropos* 18–19 (4–6): p. 684, 1923–4.

22. J.H.Soga,*The South-Eastern Bantu* (Johannesburg, 1930) pp. 59–60.

23. T. Soga in Chalmers (1877), pp. 355–6. cf. the Zulu version in T. B. Jenkinson, *Amazulu* (London, 1882) pp. 15–16.

24. T. Bain, 'The Distribution of Animals, etc., after the Creation, as related by a Kafir', *S.A. Folk-Lore Journal* II (part 2): pp. 21–3, March 1880. See Appendix I.

25. W. K. Kaye, 'Of the Creation of People', MS 172c, n.d., Grey Collection, South African Library, pp. 157–164. See Appendix II. The reference to the moon may be of Khoi origin. Grevenbroek (1965), p. 207, notes that when the moon is full, Khoi women 'who are in their monthly courses blame it for their illness'.

26. A. Kropf and R. Godfrey, *A Kafir-English Dictionary* (2nd ed. edited by R. Godfrey, Lovedale, 1915) p. 154.

27. C. M. Doke and B. W. Vilakazi, *Zulu-English Dictionary* (Johannesburg, 1948) p. 319. See also J. W. Colenso, *Zulu-English Dictionary* (Pietermaritzburg, 1884) p. 201; J. L. Döhne, *A Zulu-Kaffir Dictionary* (Cape Town, 1857) p. 126. For a discussion on the meaning of *uhlanga* see H. Callaway,

The Religious System of the Amazulu (Springdale, 1870) pp. 1–2, 76–7, and *Nursery Tales, Traditions and Histories of the Zulus* (London, 1868) p. 72; W. Wanger, 'The Zulu Notion of God', *Anthropos* 21 (3–4): pp. 360–4, 1926.

28. W. C. Holden, *The Past, Present and Future of the Kaffir Races* (London, 1866) p. 299. See also J. Shooter, *The Kafirs of Natal and the Zulu Country* (London, 1857) p. 159.

29. For examples of these Zulu cosmogonic myths: W. H. I. Bleek, *Zulu Legends* (Pretoria, 1952) pp. 2–3; A. T. Bryant, *A Zulu-English Dictionary* (Marianhill, 1905) p. 758; Callaway (1870), ch. 1; D. Kidd, *The Essential Kafir* (London, 1904) pp. 100–1, quotes Hahn as suggesting that the Zulus borrowed the myth from the Hottentots; cf. the 'creation story' of the Thonga, in which the first human beings came out of the *lihlanga*, the reed, or the *nhlanga*, the marsh of reeds: H. A. Junod, *The Life of a South African Tribe* II (rev. ed., London, 1927) p. 348.

30. Derricourt (1974), p. 55. B. W. Vilakazi disputes the link of *uhlanga* with man coming out of beds of reeds, maintaining that language influences the formation of such myths. His meaning of *uhlanga* is 'original stem or ancestry; without beginning or end; eternity'. Man is thus created from original material, giving the term a very Christian meaning: 'The Oral and Written Literature in Nguni' (unpublished D.Litt. thesis, University of Witwatersrand, 1946) pp. 144–5.

31. Wikar (1779), p. 95.

32. Stow (1905), p. 130.

33. Mabona (1973), p. 6.

34. T. Hahn, *Tsuni-//Goam, the Supreme Being of the Khoi-Khoi* (London, 1881) pp. 72, 132–4.

35. Kidd (1904), p. 412.

36. B. Holt, *Joseph Williams and the Pioneer Mission to the South-Eastern Bantu* (Lovedale, 1954) pp. 33–4; S. K. Mqhayi, *U-Mqhayi wase-Ntab'ozuko* (Lovedale, 1939) pp. 64–5.

37. Hahn (1881), pp. 65, 124, 134–5, 145; I. Schapera, *The Khoisan Peoples of South Africa: Bushmen and Hottentots* (London, 1965) p. 374.

38. See notes 14 and 15.

39. Hahn (1881), pp. 122–4; W. Ten Rhyne, 'A Short Account of the Cape of Good Hope and of the Hottentots who inhabit that Region (1686)' in *The Early Cape Hottentots*, edited by I. Schapera (Cape Town, 1933) p. 141.

40. P. Kolb, *The Present State of the Cape of Good Hope* (London, 1731) p. 29.

41. Grevenbroek (1695), p. 193. Hahn (1881), p. 105, quotes from Wuras, a Korana myth, which is similar.

42. Casalis (1861), p. vii.

43. Bryant (1905), p. 130.

44. Grevenbroek (1695), p. 255.

45. B. C. Ray, *African Religions: Symbol, Ritual and Community* (New Jersey, 1976) p. 24; Nkonki (1968), pp. 42–3.

46. Nkonki (1968), pp. 52–3, 143–7.

47. Grevenbroek (1695), p. 255. cf. report of the crew of the *Stavenisse* in 1689 in Moodie (1840), p. 431.
48. A. Steedman, *Wanderings and Adventures in the Interior of Southern Africa* (London, 1835) pp. 247–8. Prof. H. W. Pahl notes that there is a cave near Queenstown, where there are some Bushman paintings, called *uDaliwe:* interview, Fort Hare, 7 August 1981.
49. Derricourt (1974), p. 56.
50. W. Gqoba, 'The Native Tribes, their Laws, Customs and Beliefs', *Christian Express* XV (179): p. 93, 1 June 1885.
51. Kropf and Godfrey (1915), p. 294.
52. Interview with Prof. H. W. Pahl, Fort Hare, 7 August 1981. In his analysis of the traditional religion of the Rwanda people, A. Kagame develops a philosophical system based on the linguistic stem *-ntu* as being the cosmic universal force: 'La philosophie bantu rwandaise de L'être' (Ph.D. thesis, Rome, 1956). This concept has been taken up by J. Jahn as the basis for his book: *Muntu: An Outline of the New African Culture* (New York, 1961) p. 101.
53. Derricourt (1974), p. 55.
54. One of the exceptions is E. Moorcroft, 'Theories of Millenarianism considered with reference to certain South African Movements' (unpublished B.Letters, Oxford, 1967).
55. E.g. For Nxele: Kropf and Godfrey (1915), p. 499; T. Pringle, *Narrative of a Residence in South Africa* (London, 1835) p. 281; J. H. Soga, *The South-Eastern Bantu* (Johannesburg, 1930) pp. 161–2. For Nongqawuse and Mhlakaza: C. Brownlee, *Reminiscences of Kaffir Life and History* (Lovedale, 1896) ch. 1; A. Burton, 'The Cattle-Killing Movement 1856–57' (Lecture at Grahamstown, 1946, Cory Library, Rhodes University) p. 3; Nkonki (1968), pp. 199–201; Tiyo Soga in Chalmers (1877), pp. 103 *et seq.* For a general discussion: Moorcroft (1967); R. D. Ralston, 'Xhosa Cattle Sacrifice, 1856–57: The Messianic Factor in African Resistance' in *Profiles in Self-Determination. African Responses to European Colonialism in Southern Africa 1652-Present*, edited by D. Chanaiwa (Northridge, 1976) ch. 3.

4. MYTHS ABOUT THE COMING OF DEATH

Traditional Xhosa Concepts Relating to Misfortune

In the traditional world-view there is no such thing as chance. The belief system is explanatory, in a closed system of cause and effect, and 'suffering is linked with wrongdoing and so made meaningful and endurable'.[1] Anything which disturbs the harmony has a cause and has to be accounted for. Divination is used to interpret the causes of misfortune and to prescribe the means of restoring the harmony. As Hammond-Tooke observes, the signs of disturbance are 'immediate, obvious and physical. Sickness, misfortune, drought, are all signs that the balance has been upset, and one of the main objects of religious ritual and the resort to divination and protective magic is to restore it'.[2]

Although it is believed that misfortune can be caused either by ritual impurity, the breaking of a taboo, a curse, or even in certain cases 'sent' by the supreme being, it is generally thought of as being caused either by the ancestors or by witchcraft and sorcery.[3] Ancestrally sent misfortune is regarded as being a punishment for wrong doing, usually for some breach of tradition or custom and is not generally fatal. Witchcraft and sorcery, on the other, hand, are both entirely evil and can be the cause of death.

Much has been written about witchcraft and sorcery.[4] Suffice it to say that a witch is the embodiment of evil and is thought to carry out her nefarious work through a familiar or agent of harm. This can take the form of an animal such as a baboon, wildcat or owl: or a mythical being such as a *thikoloshe*, *ichanti*, *impundulu* or *zombie*. Sorcery is based on the belief that a neutral power resides in certain material substances which can be manipulated for good or evil ends. A herbalist is a person who treats with 'medicines' for protection and cure, while a sorcerer manipulates the power in the material substances for harm. Summing up, Hammond-Tooke says: 'Both religious and witchcraft beliefs are utilized to explain and control misfortune but . . . it is the witch beliefs which more specifically handle the problem of evil in the universe.'[5]

Berglund notes that there are essentially two concepts of

death: 'Firstly, a timely death which presupposes a number of children and grandchildren who survive the deceased. Secondly, there is death which is untimely and is regarded as a serious interference in a human's life.' [6] A timely death is expressed as a passing on, a continuance; but an untimely death is described as being a breaking-off of life, and the cause has to be established.

God's Messengers of Death

The explanation of how death originally came into the world is found in the corpus of myths which deal with the primordial separation between man and the supreme being. According to these myths, separation sometimes occurred as a result of man's disobedience in breaking a commandment or as an accident, but the most usual form of the myth is the one found among the Xhosa, which tells of God's messengers of death. [7]

Variations of this myth are found throughout Africa with different animals being cast in the role of the messengers of death. [8] Among the Xhosa it is told as 'The Story of the Chameleon and Lizard – *Intsomi Yolovane Nentulo*'. It looks back to a Golden Age and explains the coming of suffering, illness and death. There are three basic variants to this myth, which probably point to differences in social and religious experience and reflects an ambivalence in conceptualization of deity. In the version recorded from the oral tradition of the amaNgqika branch of the Xhosa by Nkonki, the loss of paradise is brought about by the spiteful mischief of a lizard and the 'Creator' remains in a neutral position.

> *Qamata* (the supreme being) sent the chameleon to the earth to come and tell the people that they would never die. The chameleon journeyed to the earth and on the way it got tired and had a rest. There came a lizard and it asked where the chameleon was going and the chameleon told it. The lizard ran and told the people that they would die.
>
> There arose a big outcry on the earth, people were crying because they were going to die. The chameleon heard this outcry and then proceeded to the earth to tell the people that there was nothing like that, they would never die.

33

The people never believed the chameleon; they said they had stuck to the word of the lizard. That is why people die.[9]

A similar version was recorded among the Khoi in 1779 except that the hare and the bush-tick are the messengers involved.[10]

Tiyo Soga collected a second form of the myth in the 1860s. Here the 'Creator' is seen as having the 'very best intentions towards the human Family', but he is always opposed by an undefined enemy of man. For example, when he created a bee, the enemy responded with a troublesome fly; when he created a swallow, the enemy imitated it with an ugly bat; similarly an eagle was opposed with the owl. The owl and the bat are regarded as familiars of witches and are thus seen as evil beings. In the story of the coming of death, the tardy chameleon sent by the 'Creator' is opposed by the swift rock-lizard of the enemy, and the 'Creator' is thus outwitted.[11] The idea of a creator of evil things, or satanic figure, is thought to be of Khoi origin and will be discussed later; but Christian influence could also be present here.

The most usual form of the myth, which is common to all the Nguni and possibly older than the other two, represents the supreme being, like nature itself, as being unpredictable and undependable. In this version the Creator is seen to change his mind. As given by Holden, it reads:

> The Great Being . . . after creating man, sent *Unwabi*, 'the chameleon', to him, to tell him he should live for ever. After Unwabi's departure, however, the Great Being repented, and sent after him *Intulo*, 'the quick-running salamander, to tell man he must die'. *Intulo*, being swifter, outran *Unwabi*, and coming to man, delivered his message; but man answered him: 'Go thou; we have already accepted the message which *Intulo* has brought us'. 'And so it is,' says the tradition, 'that men die.'[12]

This myth has given rise to the Xhosa proverb, 'I have already received the word of the lizard', which is roughly equivalent to 'first come first served'.[13]

Analysing this myth, Ngubane suggests that it symbolizes

34

the right of people to make decisions and to take responsibility for their actions. With regard to the symbolic role of the animals, the lizard, which is greyish-brown in colour, is black in the ritual sense and is the messenger of death. This can be associated with the idea of black 'medicines' believed to be used by the sorcerer to harm and even kill his victim. The chameleon is known for its ability to change colour to suit its surroundings and is the animal of deceiving.[14] Both animals are considered unlucky and are even hated. According to Xhosa diviners, the lizard and the chameleon are messengers of the witch sent to kill.[15]

In this myth the supreme being exhibits the same sort of ambivalence found in the divinities of ancient Semitic religions. He is both benevolent and malevolent, and with it all unpredictable. Cumpsty argues that this is because he is drawn from nature which is itself both creator and destroyer, and above all unpredictable. In his fight for survival, primal man needs both aspects in his gods, the aim being to direct the destructive power toward his enemies and the benevolent aspect toward himself. This is achieved by man interacting with the divine through ritual.[16] The Xhosa believe that *iNkosi yezulu* (the-Lord-of-the-Sky) is beneficient in sending rain to the earth, but he withholds rain if he is angry or irritated and sends lightning which kills. The ritual propitiation of the supreme being in times of drought is one of the rare occasions in which he is approached directly in worship.

McVeigh maintains that a paradoxical combination of God's attributes is resolved in the African view by pushing him to the periphery of life, and this is achieved through myth. The near God is intolerable and is therefore thrust to the periphery so as to make life bearable. The myths not only tell of man's separation from God, but they also fix his absence into the consciousness of African thought. The problem is that in times of crisis, like war, drought or epidemic disease, which are beyond the explanation and control of the ancestors, man has no recourse but to approach God himself.[17] McVeigh concludes, however, that in the final analysis God is still far away and the myths of separation remain valid.[18]

I, however, would simply want to deny that there is any

paradox here. In a nature religion, experience is essentially cyclical, and therefore creation and destruction go hand in hand as in nature itself. Furthermore, it is monistic and one normally belongs to the totality by belonging to that which is closest, which in turn belongs to that which is beyond it. It is only when the chain is somehow broken that one needs immediate recourse to that which is beyond.

Khoisan Myths of Primordial Death

In addition to the myth of the coming of death which involves the hare outwitting the bush-tick or louse, the Khoisan have a body of myths of primordial death which introduce the concept of dualism. There are different versions but they revolve around the death of the chief of the first race of man. This caused the separation of two shadows or presences of the chief to which are related the dualistic concepts of light and darkness, night and day, sky and earth, male and female, good and evil, and life and death.[19] Khoi mythology is also rich in myths incorporating the theme of resurrection; San mythology is less so. In these myths the supernatural beings and the heroes come to life many times after death, as well as resurrecting people thrown into a hole by the evil being.[20]

Amongst the Khoisan people, therefore, the problems of life and death, good and evil, are explained by the various myths, and this is reflected in their burial rites. At death the corpse was taken out through a hole at the back of the hut and then buried.[21] The grave is said to have been considered symbolically as the hole from which man originally emerged; and the various rites, such as facing the corpse east, correspond with this cosmology. Sunrise was regarded as a perpetual resurrection, hence the prayers facing eastward at dawn and other rituals by which the Khoi identified with and participated in the event.[22]

The Xhosa, on the other hand, had no myth of primordial death. They believed that they were immortal, or rather, amortal, i.e. an original total absence of death. This is said to be the reason why they did not bury their dead except for the chiefs, for with no story of primordial death there is no understanding of the first ancestral being returning to the hole of origin.[23]

The corpses of commoners were left exposed in the veld to be devoured by beasts of prey, and only the chiefs were buried in the cattle kraal.[24] The burial rites of the chiefs were very similar to those of the Khoi and could well have been incorporated from them at least in part.[25] In the 1810s, Nxele's injunction to the Xhosa to bury all their dead could have been as much the influence of his San wives and Khoi cultural diffusion, as of Christianity.[26] Certainly the resurrection beliefs which were expressed in the new ritual performances found no correspondence in Xhosa mythology.

This evidence lends support to the theory that the gradual incorporation of Khoisan elements into the Xhosa religious tradition, more especially the ritualistic approach to the supreme being, the dualistic concept of good and evil, and the idea of resurrection, was part of an ongoing process of religious change which incidentally prepared the way for Christianity. At the same time, the mythopoeic world-views of the Khoisan and Xhosa lacked any sense of eschatology. In the Khoisan system 'the resurrections are part of the cosmic process; they are taking place all the time and can be ritually influenced'.[27] It was only with the development of a linear concept of time that it became possible for African thought to conceive of the Christian notion of divine intervention in history and an end to the present order.

NOTES AND REFERENCES

1. Wilson (1971), p. 54.
2. Hammond-Tooke (1974), p. 335.
3. See Fig. 3 in B. A. Pauw, *Christianity and Xhosa Tradition* (London, 1975) p. 61.
4. E.g. A.-I. Berglund, *Zulu Thought-Patterns and Symbolism* (London, 1976) ch. 7; Hammond-Tooke (1974), pp. 335-9; Pauw (1975), ch. 11.
5. Hammond-Tooke (1974), p. 335.
6. Berglund (1976), p. 79.
7. For a general discussion on the different forms of these myths of separation see Mbiti (1970), ch. 15.
8. See for example: U. Beier, *The Origin of Life and Death* (London, 1976) pp. 32-7.
9. Nkonki (1968), p. 51.
10. Wikar (1779), pp. 139-40; Schapera (1965), pp. 357-8.

11. T. Soga in Chalmers (1877), pp. 356–8. Casalis (1861), p. 242, recorded a similar myth among the Sotho.
12. Holden (1866), p. 299. There are numerous Zulu versions of this myth. In these the chameleon wastes time by stopping to eat red berries on the way: e.g. Callaway (1870), pp. 3, 138; A. Gardiner, *Narrative of a Journey to the Zoolu country in South Africa* (London, 1836) p. 178; L. H· Samuelson, *Some Zulu Customs and Folk-Lore* (London, 1912) p. 66; Shooter (1857), p. 159; Wanger (1926), pp. 351–2, 665. cf. Thonga: Junod (1927), pp. 350–1.
13. *Zonnebloem College Magazine* 3(12): pp. 9–10, Easter, 1905.
14. H. Ngubane, *Body and Mind in Zulu Medicine* (London, 1977) p. 134.
15. M. Hirst, personal communication, 8 October 1981.
16. J. S. Cumpsty, 'Report on the C.P.S.A. Commission to Investigate the Pastoral, Practical, Theological Challenge posed by Marxism in Africa' (unpublished MS, U.C.T., 1981). See also Vilakazi (1946), p. 148.
17. According to Fr A. Fischer, where many clans are affected by drought, it cannot be that all the ancestors of all the clans have inflicted this misfortune on the people. Therefore this misfortune is beyond the control of the ancestors and that is why they go to God directly: Personal communication, 1 March 1982.
18. M. J. McVeigh, *God in Africa. Conceptions of God in Africa Traditional Religion and Christianity* (Massachusetts, 1974) pp. 128–49. See also J. A. van Wyk, 'God: Near and Far. The Question of the Resting God in Africa', *Theologia Viatorum* 1(1): pp. 28–38, Nov. 1973.
19. Mabona (1973), pp. 7–18.
20. For *Tsui//Goab*, p. 378, and *Heitsi Eibib*, p. 384, in Schapera (1965).
21. O. Dapper, 'Kaffraria or the Land of the Kafirs, also named Hottentots (1668)' in *The Early Cape Hottentots*, edited by I. Schapera (Cape Town, 1933) p. 63; Ten Rhyne (1686), p. 127; Grevenbroek (1695), pp. 259–61; Kolb (1731), pp. 313–4.
22. Mabona (1973), pp. 10–18.
23. Ibid., pp. 12–13.
24. Alberti (1810), pp. 93–6; J. Barrow, *An Account of Travels in the Interior of Southern Africa in the Years 1797 and 1798* II (2 vols., London, 1801 and 1804) pp. 220–1; Campbell (1815), p. 368; Brownlee, pp. 120–2, and Warner, pp. 102–4, in Maclean (1858); Shaw (1860), p. 428; J. H. Soga, *The Ama-Xosa: Life and Customs* (Lovedale, n.d., c. 1931) pp. 152–3, 318–24.
25. Grevenbroek (1695), pp. 259–61; Dugmore in Maclean (1858), pp. 165–6.
26. Dugmore in Maclean (1858), p. 165; G. M. Theal, *Kaffir Folk Lore* (London, 1882) p. 200.
27. Mabona (1973), p. 19.

PART III

5. NGUNI PRAISE-NAMES OF THE SUPREME BEING

'The Great Being' and his Praise-names

The traditional concept of the supreme being has been a subject of debate for many years, the argument being that because the Xhosa lacked a clearly defined belief or system of worship, the concept was of alien origin, if present at all. Undoubtedly there is ample evidence to show Khoisan influence, and the idea could well have been introduced through contact with whites prior to the missionaries' coming; but what are regarded as the traditional Xhosa praise-names of deity indicate a concept that pre-dates this cultural interaction. On the other hand, the divine titles only minimally describe the nature and attributes of the supreme being, identifying him as *fons et origo;* and he is typically the background god of a nature religion.

Whether or not the Xhosa believed in God was a controversial subject from the start of their interaction with whites, the earliest written sources being divided in their opinion. For example, Alberti (1807) is adamant that they had no conception of 'an invisible Being, to whom they ascribe a powerful influence over themselves or nature in general'.[1] While others, like Le Vaillant (1780–85),[2] Damberger (1781–97)[3] and Lichtenstein (1803–6), maintain that they at least believed 'in some sort of great Being who created the world'.[4] Campbell (1813) considers that 'even this feeble ray of light' was the result of 'intercourse with the Dutch boors (farmers) during several ages'.[5] One and all agreed, however, that the Xhosa had no religious ceremonies, places of worship or priests, as understood in Christianity. Rose (1829) sums up the prevailing white attitude when he says that they did not appear to possess religion; but only 'some wild idea of a Being that breathes his anger in the thunder, and in the famine that follows drought'.[6] Barrow obtained more explicit information when he questioned Ngqika, the Rharhabe paramount chief, in 1798:

> The king being asked if they had any belief in a supernatural power, and, if so, what were their notions con-

cerning it? replied, that they believed in the existence of some invisible power that sometimes brought good and sometimes evil upon them; it was this power that caused men to die suddenly, or before they arrived at years of maturity; that raised the wind, and made thunder and lightning to frighten, and sometimes, kill them; that led the sun across the world in the day, and the moon by night; and that made all those things which they could not understand nor imitate.[7]

Van der Kemp, who was the first missionary among the Xhosa, from 1799 to 1801, is widely quoted as saying that the Xhosa had no word in their language 'to express the deity'. Those who had some notion of his existence had 'received (it) from adjacent nations',[8] and they used the name *Tuikwa* or *Thiko* (*Thixo*) which they had 'borrowed from the Hottentots'.[9] This gives some indication of the extent of Khoi influence at this stage, and would also reflect Van der Kemp's dependence on a Khoi elephant-hunter as interpreter.

Although most of these early writers established that the Xhosa had some notion of 'a great Being', who was associated with origin and who manifested awesome power, their failure to ascertain any of the praise-names of the supreme being is not surprising in that reverence for the name of deity made casual mention of it taboo.[10] I suggest that it was only as a result of missionary influence during the early part of the 19th century that this tradition changed.

In the African tradition eulogies of important people take the form of praise-poetry or *izibongo*, and 'the different praises of a chief are frequently used as variations for his name'.[11] The praises are characterized by highly figurative language because praise of a person 'is not something to be expressed in bold or straightforward language'.[12] Rather, wide use is made of allusion and imagery, more especially metaphor.[13] Among the Nguni the God-names are similarly construed, each praise-name being 'descriptive of some particular characteristic which one wishes to emphasize when using the praise-name'.[14]

The God-names in this study are discussed under separate headings, the first group being those that are common to both Xhosa and Zulu-speaking people (Cape Nguni and Northern

Nguni). Even though the earliest information is taken from 19th century sources, the informants were often said to be 'very old' and they 'merely repeated what they had been told by "their old people", parents and grandparents', so that the chain of tradition could lead a hundred or more years back.[15] The fact that the two different branches of the Nguni used identical praise-names, that these praise-names were reported by a number of authorities to be well-established in their respective areas, that they were associated with the same attributes of the supreme being in each case, and that they are not associated with any Khoisan God-names, seems to be sufficient evidence to show that they date from before the time the Xhosa broke away from the parent Nguni body. In other words, they are traditional praise-names of the Nguni which at the least pre-date Khoisan and missionary influence, and could well be of ancient origin. Comparative evidence from various other African societies supports this view as it shows that other indigenous people have similar traditional praise-names of deity and these are also thought to be of ancient origin.[16]

uDali, uMdali and uMenzi

uDali, *uMdali* and *uMenzi* are used by both the Xhosa and the Zulu to refer to origin and creation. In Xhosa, *uDali* and *uMdali* are derived from *ukudala*, to make, bring into existence, create, ordain, appoint; and mean the creator, moulder, maker.[17] The difference between these praise-names of the supreme being is that *uDali* is only used to refer to deity, while *uMdali* is used generally as well.[18] *uMenzi* is from *ukwenza*, to make, act, bring a thing to pass; and means worker, doer, the maker of all things, the one who brings things about.[19]

Shaw (1860) observes that 'before Missionaries and other Europeans had intercourse with the Kaffirs, they seem to have had extremely vague and indistinct notions concerning the existence of God. The older Kaffirs used to speak of *Umdali*, the Creator or Maker of all things, and *Uhlanga* . . . .'[20] Döhne (1844) and Holden (1866) recorded the God-names *u Mdali* and *uMenzi* too; but while Holden claimed that they were traditional, Döhne maintained that they were of more recent origin, having being introduced by the missionaries.[21] Later evidence, but taken from the oral tradition, comes from J. H. Soga (c. 1931), who states that *uDali* was originally used by the Xhosa to denote 'the author of all existent life, the creator of man, the animals, and all forms of living things'.[22]

Kay (1833) notes that the Mpondo also used *uMdali* and *uMenzi* in a sacred sense to refer to 'that Being by whom all the great works of nature were produced – the heavens, the earth, and the sea, etc.' [23] But Hunter, who made an anthropological study of the Mpondo a hundred years later, contends that although these two names might support a belief in a creator, the absence of any system of rites or complex of beliefs indicates that the idea of a supreme being is foreign to Xhosa tradition.[24]

uMdali and *uMenzi* have the same derivations and meanings as praise-names of the supreme being in Zulu as they do in Xhosa, i.e. Creator and Maker.[25] In a discussion on the different Zulu God-names, Callaway (1870) confirms that *Unkulunkulu* (a God-name literally meaning the Great-Great One) is also called *uMenzi*, 'because he is supposed to have made all things'. However, Callaway gives the meaning of *uMdali* as 'the breaker off, because he is supposed to have been the instrumental agent by which all things were broken off or separated from the source or place of being', the reference being to the reed myth of origin.[26]

Schneider (1891), possibly following Döhne, also claimed that *uMdali* and *uMenzi* were introduced to the Xhosa by the missionaries.[27] Wanger contests this view, arguing that these were traditional Zulu God-names, and, therefore, 'considering that the Xosas [Xhosa] are the next sister, if not daughter-nation to the Zulu, the probability stands in favour of these names having been traditional also among the Xosas'.[28] He quotes Shaw to support his argument so bringing us full circle. Wanger goes on to present a lengthy philological discussion on *uMdali* and *uMenzi*, which affirms his contention that they are traditional praise-names of the supreme being, as well as discussing their usage.[29] Berglund confirms that they are common God-names which traditionalist Zulu use to this day.[30]

Recent research among the Xhosa has shown that while *uMdali* and *uMenzi* may still be linked to the concept of a creator, nowadays these words are equally applicable to human capacities and are commonly used in this context in ordinary speech.[31] Be that as it may, Pauw's Xhosa informant, an urban Anglican preacher, was adamant that '*ukudala* is an activity performed by God alone';[32] and Wanger has similar evidence for the Zulu: 'no Zulu will consciously predicate *ukudala* of a human being'.[33]

Comparative evidence provided by Mbiti indicates 'that practically all African peoples consider God as creator, making this the commonest attribute of the works or activities of God. The concept is expressed through saying directly that God created all things, through giving him the name of Creator (or its equivalent), and through addressing him in prayer as the Creator or Maker'.[34] This is well illustrated in the material which Mbiti has collected from nearly three hundred African societies.[35] An historical dimension is provided by Livingstone, who found in his travels in Southern and South-Central Africa in the 1850s, that the indigenous people he met generally believed in 'one maker of heaven and earth', and named him as their creator.[36]

uHlanga

Another praise-name associated with origin is *uHlanga*. It is linked with the cosmogonic myth concerning *uhlanga*, the cavern in the east, 'the source or place from whence all living things came forth'.[37] Of interest in this connection is the information which Callaway obtained on a journey through Kaffraria in 1875. He reports that when 'an educated, intelligent native' of the amaNgqika was asked about the origin of things before the missionaries came, he replied: '*Inyange ka'Nyange* is *Uhlanga. Uhlanga* sprang from *Uhlanga* (*ohlangeni*). He came out of a hole.'[38] *amaNyange* means the people of old, ancestors.[39] Callaway translates it as a Great-Great-Grandfather and says that it is equivalent to the Zulu *Unkulunkulu*.[40] *Inyange ka'nyange* is said to mean the Great-Great-Grandfather of the Great-Great-Grandfather, so referring the act of creation to a far remote ancestor and intending to carry creation as far back as possible from the present. The idea of *uHlanga* issuing out of *uHlanga* is readily understood in terms of the myth.

Sawyerr uses West African material to support his thesis that because God is the source of man's life he is therefore his Ancestor.[41] Early Xhosa sources seem to agree with this view, although the supposition hinges on semantics and is debatable. Kay (1833)[42] gives an account of Xhosa genealogy which names *uHlanga* or *Thlanga* as the oldest of their kings, by whose name they always swore in former days: a custom which obtained universally in the interior, according to Moffat.[43] At the same time, Kay reported that the Kaffrarian people appeared to acknowledge a divine power as being the maker of the world and the disposer of all events, whom they called *uHlanga*, the Great Spirit. But Kay said that their ideas were faint and confused, and there was no understanding of Spirit in the Christian sense: 'they had no conception of any deity but what was corporeal.'[44]

Bennie (1822) records that *Ruthlanga* was the name for the Great Being who made the sun, moon and stars; and suggests that the word was derived from *langa*, the sun.[45] But there does not appear to be such a linguistic connection, neither is the sun personified by the Xhosa as a divinity as with some African societies,[46] nor did they address it in prayer as did the San.[47]

Although the praise-name *uHlanga* was generally associated with deity as being located in the underworld, this term also referred to a power coming from the above which manifested itself in the elements.[48] So, for example, Brownlee observed in 1827, that the Xhosa 'conceive that thunder proceeds from the direct operation of Deity; and if a person is killed by lightning they say that God (*Uhlanga*) has been amongst them'.[49]

Callaway sums up the early evidence for the Zulu by saying:

> There can be no doubt that whilst *Uthlanga* is used by some to mean a reed, which is supposed to have given origin to all things; and others speak of *Uthlanga* as the place from which all things came out,[50] yet the majority give it a personal signification; and in tracing the tradition backwards, we rest at last in *Uthlanga* as the word which of all others has wrapped up in it the native idea of a Creator.[51]

Wanger (1926) notes that *uHlanga* is the original form of this

God-name among the Zulus but that it can also figure as *uLuh-langa*. He concludes that 'the name *uHlanga* is not primarily a God-name, but only applied to Him, although, the application once made, He is in the native mind "the" *uHlanga*, "the" Origin'.[52] Wanger maintains that all those authors who regarded *uHlanga* as one of the principal Xhosa and Zulu God-names gave it undue importance.[53] Berglund found that *uHlanga* is still used as a praise-name of the supreme being among the Zulu of today.[54]

Mbiti provides comparable God-names in other African societies. Of particular interest is the fact that the Ngoni of Malawi use *Uluhlanga* to mean 'the Original Source';[55] and this was recorded as early as 1857 by Döhne.[56]

iNkosi yezulu

Traditional Xhosa thought-patterns about the above indicate that the supreme being was closely associated with the sky, just as in classical mythological thought, and was sometimes even called the sky, *iZulu*.[57] All the awesome and more dangerous aspects of nature, such as drought, thunder, lightning, hail, violent rain and wind, were attributed to the supreme being and were often personified by *iZulu*. Comparative material drawn from other African societies shows that this is one of the most common conceptualizations of deity.[58] When lightning struck a person the Xhosa say *'izulu limthabathile'* ('the sky has taken him'),[59] or *'watatyatwa lizulu'* ('he was taken by heaven').[60] *Izulu liyaduduma* literally means 'the heaven thunders'.[61]

Lightning was also conceived as a bird, *impundulu* or *intake-zulu*, the bird of heaven. Thunder was the beating of its wings.[62] Ideas about the mythical lightning-bird are rich and varied, and are a feature of Xhosa folk-lore.[63] *Impundulu* was said to be dazzling in the brilliance of its different colours. Superstition held that it set its fat on fire and sent it down as lightning. Where this struck it left its eggs. These resembled hen's eggs and were thought to bring bad luck to the neighbourhood where they were laid. The bird was also supposed to be used in witchcraft as a familiar. Certain women were believed to have received an *impundulu* from an ancestor, with which they could work

47

harm on others.[64] Another lively belief was that *impundulu* was the servant of the supreme being, and was greatly feared as a messenger of death.[65]

Lightning was also sometimes referred to as *Inkosi* (Shaw 1860),[66] a term denoting respect and authority which was formerly restricted to chiefs of royal blood;[67] *Inkosi Enkulu* [*Enkhulu*] (Döhne 1844), Great Chief,[68] and *Inkosi Yezulu* [*iNkosi yezulu*] Chief or Lord-of-the-Sky.[69] This explains Warner's (1858) misconception that lightning was traditionally thought of as being governed by 'the ghost of the greatest and most renowned of their departed Chiefs'.[70]

A custom that has been handed down over the ages is for everybody to sit down quietly when there is thunder and lightning as it is believed that *iNkosi yezulu* is speaking.[71] Again when someone is struck by lightning the Xhosa say: '*ufekethelwe yiNkosi*' or '*udlalwe yiNkosi*', which both mean 'the Lord has played with him'.[72] The Khoi also spoke of a Great Chief in the sky, and lightning and thunder were said to be manifestations of his anger.[73]

In the 1930s, Hunter's Mpondo informants maintained that *iNkosi yezulu* was 'only an *ukuhlonipha*, a polite mode of reference to something that is feared'; and, as with the other praise-names already mentioned, she could find no system of belief or practices associated with *iNkosi yezulu*.[74] However, Berglund's work on the Zulu concept of the Lord-of-the-Sky has since convinced her that the Nguni people had a traditional belief in the supreme being, albeit shadowy.[75]

There is a large body of material on Zulu notions of *iNkosi yezulu*, past and present. Colenso (1855) gives one of the earliest references,[76] while Callaway (1870) devotes a whole section to the subject.[77] As with the Xhosa tradition there is the link between *iNkosi yezulu* and thunder and lightning. A traditional phrase commonly used by Zulus during a thunderstorm was that 'the Lord is playing',[78] and when someone was struck by lightning they would say, 'the Lord is angry'.[79]

Wanger analyses Callaway's evidence to show the great age of the name *iNkosi yezulu*. Furthermore, he maintains that proof of the great age and general importance of this God-name comes from the fact that 'the Zulus take their most solemn oath by "the Lord in Heaven", more solemn even than that by the living king (*inkosi*)'.[80] Wanger goes on to say:

> Comparatively modern heathenism ascribes power over lightning and hail to the magician or witch (*umtaki*). But the older traditional belief in the Lord in Heaven is still so strong that, if someone has been killed by lightning, the natives will, in naive inconsequence, say in one breath 'So-and-so has been taken by the Lord', and 'So-and-so had the lightning sent to him by So-and-so' (the supposed male or female witch).[81]

During his research in Natal and Zululand in the 1920s, Wanger found that in some parts it was thought that if a person was struck by lightning, 'the Lord had found fault with him or her'. In other parts, however, it was believed that it was a distinction to be 'taken by the Lord' in this way.[82]

Berglund gives a comprehensive description of present-day Zulu concepts of the Lord-in-the-Sky; but while it is far more detailed than anything given by Callaway and other 19th century writers, the numerous correspondences between contemporary and earlier evidence testify to deeply rooted traditions.[83] Comparative evidence from the African societies examined by Mbiti shows that practically all African people 'associate God with the heavens, sky or firmament, in one way or another'.[84]

Rituals associated with *iNkosi yezulu*

The rituals associated with *iNkosi yezulu* all have to do with his manifestation in the form of lightning. Van der Kemp provides the earliest written evidence among the Xhosa. Sometime between 1799 and 1801 he collected the strange tradition that during great thunderstorms a man dressed in green was supposed to be seen in Xhosa kraals. It was said that he always leant against the stump of a tree, having his eyes fixed on the ground. He refused all offers of hospitality and would neither eat their food nor enter their homes. He seldom spoke, but once during a violent storm he was heard to say: 'Do not be afraid, I only play with this country!' The Xhosa called him 'the Lord from above, *Pezoulo* [*Phezulu*]'. When he was seen in a kraal, the people immediately vacated it, leaving every-

49

thing behind. They then slew some beasts and put on new clothes.[85]

Anything which was struck by lightning, whether man, beast or dwelling, was considered to have become impure and it became obligatory to summon the traditional doctor to treat the object or person ritually with medicine of purification.[86] Uncleanness is evidence of disorder; hence the order must be restored. One way of doing this is to purify with medicines and another is to abstain from taking certain foods or to fast (*ukuzila*).[87]

With regard to the concept of uncleanness, Fischer observes that according to present-day beliefs, someone struck by lightning is thought to have been affected by power and the doctoring by the *igqirha* is to protect the person from being struck again, by getting the power out of him. His informant told him that 'if they are not treated they shrivel up, become bent, dry out and die'.[88]

Brownlee (1858) records that because lightning was regarded as the direct operation of the supreme being, the object or person struck was considered as having been directly appropriated to himself. Heaven had taken its own, and it was therefore wrong to murmur or complain and there was no mourning or lamentation. Instead, after the purification, the person's death was made 'a cause of dancing and rejoicing'.[89] Callaway records similar beliefs and practices among the Zulu.[90]

According to Brownlee, the fines paid for the non-observance of the customs in connection with the striking of lightning went to the chief. The kraal was deserted, the huts were allowed to fall down, and the kraal might not be used for fuel, though a scarcity of wood might exist.[91] He maintains that after the purification ritual there was a sacrificial killing to propitiate the supreme being, *Izulu*. Although he never personally observed a whole burnt offering being made at this ritual, he was told that Qatsi (Mngqatsi), who acted as 'priest rain maker and witch doctor' to Ngqika during the 1810s,[92] occasionally sacrificed an animal, the whole of which was burnt. The people of the surrounding villages furnished the fuel. Brownlee is adamant that this sacrifice was to propitiate the supreme being and not the ancestral spirits, as was the usual practice;[93] and his evidence gains credibility by being corroborated by other informants.

Shaw (1860) also notes that ritual killings were customarily directed towards the ancestral spirits, and that the sacrificial rite following a person's death by lightning was the only occasion on which it was offered to *Nkosi*. He further observes that it occurred rather frequently during the summer months in some parts of Kaffraria, which of course is in the summer rainfall region.[94]

Brownlee believed that the burial of animals killed by lightning was in the nature of a whole offering too, and suggested that the reason they were not burnt was because 'the fire of heaven' had already been on them.[95] Fischer contests this view, arguing that animals killed by lightning are buried where they are struck because they are regarded as being contaminated. Thus they are not seen as an offering.[96] This idea corresponds with the Zulu information as set down by Wanger.[97]

The other references to ritual killings being directed to the supreme being differ somewhat in detail but they nonetheless show that such a sacrifice undoubtedly took place, which disputes the assertion that no rituals were directed to the worship of the supreme being. I of course use the word worship in the broader sense for any relationship with deity, which might manifest on different occasions as invocation, appeasement, restoration of harmonious relationship, as well as the simple expression of adoration.

Döhne (1844) states that he obtained his information from a few old people. They said that because *Inkosi Enkulu* manifested his wrath with them by killing men or cattle with his lightning, he had to be appeased with a sacrifice so that he would not send down his wrath again on that same place. A special cow was slaughtered and immolated, and they would say, 'Heaven has eaten her'.[98] This is confirmed by Bokwe (1881).[99] According to Rose (1829), when a kraal was struck by lightning, the site was either deserted, or an ox burned on the spot, or buried beneath it, as an offering to *uHlanga*, the spirit of thunder.[100] Lichtenstein (1812) relates that if this misfortune should happen to the 'king's' kraal, a hundred oxen had to be slain, and all left there. Anyone could come and take away the meat, the rest being left to the hyenas.[101]

J. H. Soga gives a detailed description of the 'purification ritual' followed when someone was killed by lightning, and of the burial procedure, including the use of protective medicine. Special measures were also taken during a severe thunderstorm to prevent lightning from striking. This involved the head of the homestead stabbing the air with an assegai, and spitting medicine in the direction of the storm. This was a symbolic ritual intended to kill the *impundulu* and so prevent it from reaching the ground.[102] Wanger[103] and Berglund[104] have collected together comparable Zulu material which contains many of the old traditions.

Cosmology

Even though the supreme power was located in the above, this did not necessarily mean high above. In traditional thinking there was little sense of a spatial dimension for heaven: it was thought to be a place in the sky not far above the clouds;[105] and without a radical gap between the background god and the realm of heaven there is no need to conceptualize heaven as remote, as an expression of the transcendence of the divine being.

The Xhosa gave scant thought to cosmology. The heavenly bodies did not intrude in their lives as did thunder and lightning, and so did not require the same sort of explanation. This is in marked contrast to the Khoisan for whom the heavenly bodies, and especially the moon, were central in worship.[106] The Xhosa only took note of a few prominent stars, the Milky Way, the sun and the moon. They were given expressive names but there was no speculation about their nature or their movement, nor were they personified.

According to J. H. Soga, the moon was an enigma to the Xhosa. A popular belief was that a fresh moon made its appearance with each and every rising, the old one ceasing to exist when it set. It was thought that the horizon of the sea was the boundary of the world, and that a huge heap of moons was stored in a vast pit beyond the horizon ready for use.[107]

There seems to be an association here with the cosmogonic myth.

The Xhosa year revolved around the agricultural cycle and the stars derived their only significance from being linked with certain daily and seasonal events in this cycle. So, for example, the evening star was associated with milking time.[108] The Pleiades, *Isilimela*, were the exception in having a metaphysical association and this may well be due to Khoi influence, but there was no comparable religious ritual.[109]

Isilimela is derived from *ukulima* which means 'to hoe in seed, to dig, plough, cultivate'.[110] The first appearance of the Pleiades above the eastern horizon at dawn each year signalled the start of the cultivation season, hence the name the 'digging-for' stars. This coincided with the month of June, named *eyesilimela*, and heralded the beginning of the Xhosa new year. Besides the symbolic link with the earth as the source of new life, *Isilimela* also symbolized new life in man for the time of the coming-out ceremony of the *abakwetha* (circumcision) school was determined by the appearance of this constellation. It has always been the custom for Xhosa men to count their years of manhood from this date.[111] While the correspondence between social and cosmic events can be regarded at one level as a simple system of indicating the passage of time, at a deeper level it can be seen as a means whereby the Xhosa entered into the rhythm of nature and so experienced the divine.

uMvelingqangi, uNkulunkulu, Mz'anzima and Utabu

Callaway collected a number of other traditional Xhosa praise-names of the supreme being during his travels through Kaffraria in 1875.[112] His orthography is outdated and his spelling and grammatical construction seem strange today. The one which he calls *umVelatanqi* is generally known as *uMvelinqangi*. This praise-name has an important connection with the 'creation narratives' of the Zulu and is possibly of Zulu origin.[113] It is derived from *ukuvela*, to come forth from, to originate; and *nqangi*, first in point of time. Among the Xhosa it is used to mean the first born, the original creator who produced existing things.[114] Berglund notes that with the Zulu it refers to the first-born of twins and that there is an association of ideas with

53

the sky. Callaway was told by a missionary among the Zulu that they applied the word *Umvelinqangi* to the heir of the chieftainship when he assumes the government on the death of his father.[115]

The God-name *uNkulunkulu* (*Nkulunkulu*) is derived from *kulu* meaning great, big, much, large[116]; and is generally understood to mean 'the Great-Great One', 'the Greatest'.[117] Callaway's information about the Xhosa use of *uNkulunkulu* is that it was a praise-name of the supreme being used by 'the northern Kafir tribes', i.e. those nearest to the Zulu-speaking people.[118] Thus among the Mpondo one tradition was that it was *Ukulukulu* [*uNkulunkulu*] 'who moulded the first men'. Another said: '*Uhlanga* delivered the great message of morality to *Ukulukulu; Ukulukulu* made *Uhlanga* (also) that it may create (*dabula*) all things.' When Callaway asked how it was that *Ukulukulu* should receive the great messages from *Uhlanga*, if *Uhlanga* was made by him, he was given the prompt reply: '*Ukulukulu* sprang from *Uhlanga*, and then made another *Uhlanga* that it might create all things.' As Callaway indicates with reference to the term *Uhlanga*, the confusion in such statements is only apparent,[119] and is better understood in relation to the cosmogonic myth.[120]

Wanger maintains that not only is *uNkulunkulu* a traditional God-name of the Xhosa, but that its tradition is substantially the same as that of the Zulu.[121] This tradition has been dealt with in detail by Callaway,[122] while Wanger gives an analysis of all the early material on the subject.[123]

Berglund claims that the term *Nkulunkulu* is applicable to both the Lord-of-the-Sky and, in its plural form, to the shades (ancestors). He says: 'It can refer to both the Lord-of-the-Sky, a particular shade, or even an old person.'[124] However, he believes that while the term *Nkulunkulu* 'encompasses an atmosphere of antiquity and age', the term Lord-of-the-Sky has priority.[125]

A more obscure God-name is *Umz'omzima* (*Umz'onzima*) which appears to be linked with *Mz'anzima*, a praise-name of the supreme being, which Callaway collected among the Mpondo.[126] *umZi* is a group of huts belonging to a single owner, dwelling or village,[127] while *nzima* has the connotation of heaviness, weight, importance.[128] Callaway gives the meaning of *Mz'anzima* as 'Thou Great Dwelling Place' and maintains that it is common in other dialects as well as the Mpondo. Explaining its metaphorical associations, he says 'they will often salute a great man, in whom they trust, by the title *Mzi wetu*, our village or dwelling place'. The literal meaning of *nzima* is weighty, heavy; but here it implies solid, full of satisfaction and joy. 'When a chief leaves his village, they say that without him it is light, that is, without stability or comfort. When he returns they say, the village is heavy, that is, established and full of satisfaction.' Callaway concludes by commenting that the figurative title, 'Great Dwelling Place', is reminiscent of 'the words of the old Hebrew, Thou art our dwelling place in all generations; or again, Be Thou my strong habitation whereunto I may resort'.[129]

According to Callaway, there were various other names applied by the Mpondo to the supreme being, all being 'expressive of antiquity and creation'. The only other one he mentions, though, is *Utabu* which he said was originally used among the Mpondo until displaced by the missionaries for *Thixo;* but in 1875 it was still a favourite appellation among the old people. No meaning is offered but it may be linked with *ntaba*, a mountain, which can be used literally to denote something standing alone. The idea of a mountain is also a popular image in the praises of a chief.[130] *Utabu* was invoked when someone sneezed, as the Xhosa did *Thixo* or *Qamata*. Callaway was given a song by Umhlangayo, a grandson of Faku, which was an invocation to *Utabu* and consisted merely of a repetition of the name, but pronounced *Tebu*, sung in two parts. The missionary was also given a prayer which they addressed to *Utabu*, the translation of which was: 'Oh *Tabu*, we pray that we may have prosperity on the earth; Thou Great Dwelling Place.'[131]

Pahl comments on the remarkable gift which the Xhosa have for bestowing praise-names or other appellations upon people, based on circumstances or characteristics. Consequently, many names have been bestowed upon God over the years by Christianized Xhosas, e.g. *uSomandla*, the Almighty, *uSonini-nanini*, He who is from Everlasting, etc., and the ones coined by

Ntsikana such as *uHlathi lenyaniso*, the Forest of Truth, *uKhaka lenyaniso*, the Shield of Truth, and *uSifuba-sibanzi*, Broad-Breast, for Christ. The list of old and new God-names numbers nearly 60 and is by no means exhausted.[132]

NOTES AND REFERENCES

1. Alberti (1810), p. 47. Hirst notes that following the Second Frontier War, Alberti was General Janssen's special representative and much, especially esoteric knowledge, may have been kept from him in his role as 'conqueror'.
2. F. Le Vaillant, *Travels into the Interior Parts of Africa by way of the Cape of Good Hope in the years 1780, 81, 82, 83, 84 and 85* II (London, 1790) p. 344.
3. C. F. Damberger, *Travels in the Interior of Africa from the Cape of Good Hope to Morocco, from the years 1781 to 1797* (London, 1801) p. 106.
4. Lichtenstein (1812–15) I: pp. 301, 311.
5. Campbell (1815), p. 365.
6. C. Rose, *Four Years in Southern Africa* (London, 1829) p. 81.
7. Barrow II (1804), p. 214.
8. J. T. van der Kemp, 'An Account of the Religion, Customs . . . of Caffraria', *Transactions of the Missionary Society* I (London, 1795–1802) p. 432.
9. J. T. van der Kemp, Entry in Journal for 15 April 1800: *Transactions* I, p. 416. See also Entry for 15 September 1799, p. 397.
10. This is discussed below under the Concept of *Qamata*.
11. J. Opland, ' "Scop" and "Imbongi" – Anglo-Saxon and Xhosa Transitional Poets', *English Studies in Africa* 14: p. 174, 1971. For a general discussion on Xhosa praise-poetry see J. Opland, 'Southeastern Bantu Eulogy and Early Indo-European Poetry' in *Research in African Literatures* 11 (3): pp. 295–307, Fall 1980.
12. R. Finnegan, *Oral Literature in Africa* (Oxford, 1970) pp. 118 and 134–5.
13. Ibid., pp. 58–9.
14. Berglund (1976), p. 35.
15. Bishop Colenso (1855) quoted by Wanger, *Anthropos* 18–19 (4–6): p. 673, 1923–1924.
16. 'List of African Peoples, their Countries and Names for God', Mbiti (1970), pp. 328–36.
17. W. J. Davis, *Dictionary of the Kafir Language* (London, 1872) p. 36; Kropf and Godfrey (1915), p. 71.
18. Interview with Prof. H. W. Pahl, Fort Hare, 8 February 1982.
19. Kropf and Godfrey (1915), pp. 95–6.
20. Shaw (1860), p. 451.
21. J. L. Döhne, *Das Kaffernland und Seine Bewohner* (Berlin, 1844) p. 55; Holden (1866), p. 299.
22. J. H. Soga (n.d.), p. 150.
23. S. Kay, *Travels and Researches in Caffraria* (London, 1833) p. 339.

24. M. Hunter, *Reaction to Conquest. Effects of Contact with Europeans on the Pondo of South Africa* (London, 1st ed. 1936, 2nd ed. 1961) p. 269.
25. Bryant (1905), p. 90; Colenso (1884), pp. 92 and 325; Döhne (1857), pp. 57–8 and 73; Doke and Vilakazi (1948), pp. 137 and 191.
16. Callaway (1870), p. 89. There is another reference to *uMdali* on p. 97. Wanger does not subscribe to Callaway's equation of *dala = dabula*, because the latter is a component of two ideas, viz. 'create' and 'break': *Anthropos* 21 (3–4): p. 357, 1926.
27. Wanger, *Anthropos* 18–19 (4–6): p. 678, 1923–4.
28. Ibid.
29. Wanger, *Anthropos* 21 (3–4): pp. 355–60, 1923–4.
30. Berglund (1976), pp. 35–6.
31. D. G. Bettison, 'The Cosmology of the Southern Bantu' (unpublished dissertation, Rhodes University, 1954) p. 4. See also E. H. Bigalke, 'The Religious System of the Ndlambe of East London District' (unpublished M. A. Thesis, Rhodes University, 1969) pp. 70–3.
32. 'The word *ukudala*, used in the Bible for the act of creating, is distinct from *ukwenza*, doing or making, and *ukwakha*, building or forming': Pauw (1975), p. 77.
33. Wanger, *Anthropos* 21 (3–4): p. 356, 1926.
34. Mbiti (1970), p. 45.
35. Ibid., pp. 45–8 and 327–36.
36. Livingstone quoted in Jenkinson (1882), p. 32. See also D. Livingstone, *Missionary Travels and Researches in South Africa* (London, 1857) pp. 158 and 641.
37. Shaw (1860), p. 451. See also Holden (1866), p. 299. J. Brownlee gives the meaning as 'Supreme', in G. Thompson, *Travels and Adventures in Southern Africa* II (London, 1827) p. 448.
38. H. Callaway, 'On the Religious Sentiment amongst the Tribes of South Africa', *The Cape Monthly Magazine* 2: pp. 92–3, 1880. The Mpondo concept of *uHlanga* is given on p. 100.
39. Kropf and Godfrey (1915), p. 303.
40. For a comprehensive discussion on the meaning of *Unkulunkulu* see Wanger (1926).
41. H. Sawyerr, *God: Ancestor or Creator? Aspects of traditional belief in Ghana, Nigeria and Sierra Leone* (London, 1970).
42. Kay (1833), p. 149.
43. Moffat (1842), p. 68.
44. Kay (1833), p. 240.
45. J. Bennie, Letter dated 20 March 1822, *Report of the Glasgow Missionary Society*, Appendix: p. 29, 1822.
46. Mbiti (1970), pp. 132–3.
47. Schapera (1965), pp. 173–7.
48. E. W. Smith (ed.), *African Ideas of God* (London, 1950) p. 101. cf. similar Sotho ideas about the location of God: K. Nürnberger, 'The Sotho Notion of the Supreme Being and the Impact of the Christian Proclamation',

Journal of Religion in Africa VII (fasc. 3): p. 184, 1975; G. M. Setiloane, *The Image of God among the Sotho-Tswana* (Rotterdam, 1976) p. 78.

49. Brownlee (1827), p. 449.
50. The best evidence of these meanings is in D. Leslie, *Among the Zulus and Amatongas* (London, 1875) p. 207; and Shooter (1857), p. 159.
51. Callaway (1870), p. 82.
52. Wanger, *Anthropos* 21 (3–4): pp. 360–1, 1926.
53. Ibid.
54. Berglund (1976), pp. 35–6.
55. Mbiti (1970), p. 333.
56. Döhne (1857), p. 672.
57. C. Brownlee, 'A fragment on Xhosa Religious Beliefs', *African Studies* 14(1): p. 38, 1955.
58. E. Dammann, 'A Tentative Philological Typology of some African High Deities', *Journal of Religion in Africa* II: pp. 81–95, 1969. See also E. Dammann, 'Die Religiöse Bedeutung des Bantuwortstammes – Lungu', *Ex Orbe Religionum* (1922) pp. 207–17; Hammond-Tooke (1974), pp. 320–1; Mbiti (1970), ch. 12.
59. J. McLaren, 'Religious Beliefs and Superstitions of the Xosas: A study in Philology', *S.A. Journal of Science* XV: pp. 421–2, 1918.
60. Brownlee, *African Studies* 14(1): p. 38, 1955.
61. Davis (1872), p. 42; Kropf and Godfrey (1915), p. 86.
62. Kidd (1904), pp. 119–20; J. H. Soga (n.d.), pp. 213–6. cf. the Bhaca – W. D. Hammond-Tooke, *Bhaca Society* (Cape Town, 1962) p. 282; Bomvana – P. A. W. Cook, *The Social Organization and Ceremonial Institutions of the Bomvana* (Cape Town, n.d.) pp. 134–5; Lovedu – E. J. and J. D. Krige, *The Realm of a Rain Queen* (London, 1943) p. 254; Thonga – Junod (1927), pp. 428–47; Zulu – Berglund (1976), pp. 38–9; Callaway (1870), pp. 117–24; General – H. P. Junod, *Bantu Heritage* (Johannesburg, 1938) pp. 134–6; Willoughby (1932), 91–6.
63. E.g. M. Bourke, *Badoli the Ox* (Cape Town, n.d.) pp. 25–9; M. L. Hewat, *Bantu Folk Lore* (Cape Town, n.d.) p. 91; A. Werner, *Myths and Legends of the Bantu* (London, 1933) ch. 15.
64. R. Godfrey, *Bird-lore of the Eastern Cape Province* (Johannesburg, 1941) pp. 2–3; Kropf and Godfrey (1915), p. 342.
65. Bokwe (1914), p. 3.
66. Shaw (1860), pp. 454–5.
67. Kropf and Godfrey (1915), p. 194.
68. Döhne (1844), p. 56. The Xhosa king was also known by this title.
69. Hunter (1961), p. 270.
70. Warner in Maclean (1866), p. 85.
71. S. Dwane, 'Christianity in relation to Xhosa religion' (unpublished Ph.D. thesis, University of London, 1979) p. 221.
72. Information from Fr. A. Fischer, personal communication, 1 March 1982.
73. Ten Rhyne (1686), pp. 139–41.
74. Hunter (1936/1961), p. 270.

75. Interview with Prof. M. Wilson (née Hunter), Hogsback, 20 July 1979.
76. J. W. Colenso, *Ten Weeks in Natal* (Cambridge, 1855) quoted in Wanger, *Anthropos* 18–19 (4–6): p. 666, 1923 – 4.
77. Callaway (1870), pp. 117–25.
78. Wanger, *Anthropos* 21 (3–4): p. 374, 1926.
79. Callaway (1870), p. 118.
80. 'The one who is taking it (the oath), either spits lightly on the tip of his right forefinger, or takes with it a little spittle from his tongue, points with it heavenwards, while saying *inKosi epezulu* "by the Lord in Heaven", and some will immediately make the gesture of cutting the throat saying *qwi*.': Wanger, *Anthropos* 21 (3–4): p. 374, 1926.
81. Ibid., pp. 374–5.
82. Ibid., p. 375. Wanger gives five other Zulu God-names connected with *iNkosi yezulu*.
83. Berglund (1976), ch. 2.
84. Mbiti (1970), p. 130. See also Dammann (1969), pp. 81–95.
85. Van der Kemp, 'An Account of the Religion. . .', *Transactions I :* p. 433.
86. Brownlee's notes, pp. 124–5, and Warner's notes, pp. 85–6, in Maclean (1858); Lichtenstein (1812–15) I: p. 318. See also J. H. Soga (n.d. *c.* 1931), pp. 213–4.
87. Kropf and Godfrey (1915), p. 489.
88. Information obtained by Fr A. Fischer from Nomawuntini Qadushe, a lady living near McKay's Nek Mission in Transkei. Dr E. Weiss of Glen Grey Hospital says that Nomawuntini's description is typical of the way people suffering from psychological problems, such as depression, describe themselves. She says that the lightning victims she has treated generally believe that lightning has been sent by an enemy, and that is why they resort to an *igqirha*, to divine the witch and to give them strength against the enemy: Personal communication, 1 March 1982. This information compares with the two Zulu traditions recorded by Wanger, the older one linking lightning with *iNkosi yezulu* and the more modern one, to a witch.
89. Brownlee in Maclean (1858), p. 125. Shaw (1860), p. 455, records 'that they do not allow any lamentation to be made for a person killed by lightning, as they say that it would be a sign of disloyalty to lament for one whom the *Inkosi* had sent for; and it would cause him to punish them by making the lightning again descend and do them another injury.'
90. Callaway (1870), pp. 117–8. For the Zulu, see also Samuelson (1912), pp. 51–2; and for the Sotho, Casalis (1861), p. 242. cf. the Nuer beliefs about the 'colwic' spirits, i.e. the people who were killed by lightning and became 'Spirits of the Above': E. E. Evans-Pritchard, *Nuer Religion* (London, 1956) pp. 52–62.
91. Brownlee in Maclean (1858), p. 125.
92. Peires dates Mngqatsi as being active as a rainmaker around 1840, after the death of Ngqika: Peires (1981), pp. 71, 74 and 165.
93. Brownlee, *African Studies* 14 (1): p. 38, 1955.
94. Shaw (1860), p. 454. Cattle burials have been excavated by archaeologists

near Middledrift in Ciskei, dating between A.D. 1670 and 1760. They are sometimes accompanied by human burials and are thought to have been carried out by pre-Nguni pastoralists, possibly as part of a funeral feast. I suggest that they could have been associated with death by lightning: Derricourt (1970), pp. 142–4, 155–9, 217.

95. Brownlee, *African Studies* 14 (1): p. 38, 1955.
96. Fischer, personal communication, 1 March 1982.
97. Wanger, *Anthropos* 21 (3–4): p. 375, 1926.
98. Döhne (1844), pp. 56–7.
99. J. K. Bokwe, 'Remarks', G. 66–'83, *Report on Proceedings with Appendices on the Government Commission on Native Laws and Customs*, 1883, Appendix B, p. 21.
100. Rose (1829), p. 145.
101. Lichtenstein (1812–15) I: p. 318.
102. There are many other practices associated with lightning: J. H. Soga (n.d.), 214–6. See also Cook (n.d.), pp. 134–7; Godfrey (1941), pp. 2–3.
103. Wanger, *Anthropos* 21 (3–4): p. 375, 1926.
104. Berglund (1976), pp. 37–42.
105. Early evidence: Callaway (1868), pp. 152–3. Later evidence: Berglund (1976), p. 32; Pauw (1975), p. 132. For African Myths and Legends about the heaven country: Werner (1933), ch. 4.
106. Schapera (1965), pp. 172–7, 374–6, 413–7.
107. J. H. Soga (n.d.), pp. 419–20. cf. Callaway (1870), p. 396; Kidd (1904), pp. 108–9.
108. It was either called *Ikwezi* or *Ucel'izapolo*, meaning 'the one who asks for a little milk from the teat'. For further information on Xhosa cosmology: J. McLaren, *A Xhosa Grammar* (London, 1940) p. 218; 'Notes on Starlore', *The Cape Quarterly Review* 1: pp. 53–5, Oct. 1881; J. H. Soga (n.d.), p. 419; Theal (1910), p. 248.
109. At the appearance of the Pleiades the Khoi mothers took their babies to an elevated spot and taught them to stretch their hands towards the 'friendly stars'. Meanwhile the people of the kraal danced and sang and prayed to *Tiqua (Tsui//Goab)* for rain and food: Schapera (1965), p. 378.
110. Kropf and Godfrey (1915), p. 216.
111. For further information on *Isilimela*: Brownlee in Thompson (1827), pp. 452–3; I. Bud-M'Belle, *Kafir Scholar's Companion* (London, 1903) p. xiv; Callaway (1870), p. 397 n. 58; Campbell (1815), p. 370; Kropf and Godfrey (1915), p. 216; J. H. Soga (n.d.), p. 419. There are comparable ideas about the Pleiades among other African people, e.g. H. Ashton, *The Basuto* (London, 1952) p. 123; Junod (1927), p. 309; E. J. Krige, *The Social System of the Zulus* (2nd ed., Pietermaritzburg, 1950) p. 190; W. C. Willoughby, *The Soul of the Bantu* (London, 1928) pp. 220–1. The early winter rising and spring setting of the Pleiades were important dates to the Farmers in Ancient Greece too.
112. Callaway, 'Religious Sentiment', *CCM* 2: pp. 99–100, 1880.
113. Berglund (1976), pp. 33–5; Wanger, *Anthropos* 21 (3–4): pp. 353–4, 1926.

114. Kropf and Godfrey (1915), pp. 451, 282. See also Davis (1872), pp. 147, 234.
115. For references to *uMvelinqangi* in the Zulu tradition: Bryant (1905), pp. 397, 444, 677–8; Colenso (1884), p. 380; Döhne (1857), p. 364; Doke and Vilakazi (1948), pp. 591, 832.
116. Kropf and Godfrey (1915), p. 199.
117. Wanger argues convincingly against the meaning as being 'the old-old one' as given by Callaway (1870), p. 1, *Anthropos* 20 (3–4): p. 569, 1925.
118. Callaway, 'Religious Sentiment', *CCM* 2: p. 99, 1880.
119. Ibid., pp. 100–1.
120. In the Zulu cosmogonic myth given by Leslie (1875), pp. 207–8, *Umvel'-nqanki* is said to have been first, and he came out of the *Uhlanga*, which literally means 'reed' but is also understood as the origin (time of origin or place of origin of all things). This *Umvel'nqanki*, 'after coming on the scene himself, brought out . . . men, women, animals, corn and all the fruits of the earth.'
121. Wanger, *Anthropos* 18–19 (4–6): p. 678, 1923–4.
122. Callaway (1870), part I.
123. Wanger, *Anthropos* 18–19 (4–6): pp. 656–87, 1923–24; 20 (3–4): pp. 558–78, 1925; 21 (3–4): pp. 351–85, 1926.
124. Berglund (1976), p. 36.
125. Ibid.
126. Callaway (1880), pp. 99, 101.
127. Döhne (1844), p. 386; Kropf and Godfrey (1915), p. 488.
128. Döhne (1844), p. 259; Kropf and Godfrey (1915), p. 310.
129. Callaway (1880), pp. 101–2.
130. Döhne (1844), p. 336; Kropf and Godfrey (1915), p. 401. *Ntaba* was the praise-name of the Xhosa paramount Sarhili (Kreli).
131. Callaway, p. 101. The words of the song were '*Ah! Tebu, Tebu, Tebu, Tebu, Tebu*', and the music was arranged for men's and women's voices. The ideophone *Tebu* means redness: Doke and Vilakazi (1948), p. 778. The colour reference could be a link with divinership or to the coming out of the young men from the circumcision lodge, when they smear their faces with red ochre; but then there is no connection with the divine. Father H. Kuckertz notes that while ancestors and things related to them are represented symbolically there is no symbolic representation of Godhead among the traditional Xhosa. Interview, Lumko, 17 October 1981.
132. Communication from Prof. H. W. Pahl, Director of the Xhosa Dictionary Project, 18 October 1978; and discussion with Prof. Pahl, Mr. O. B. Mpondo and Mr. T. A. Ndungane at Fort Hare, 8 February 1982. See Appendix III.

6. KHOISAN INFLUENCE ON THE XHOSA CONCEPT OF THE SUPREME BEING *QAMATA*

The 'borrowing' of God-names from the Khoisan

The 'borrowing' of words is an indication of a diffusion of ideas between cultures. It can shed light on the nature of their interaction and give insight into changes that have taken place in their religious history.[1] As already noted, a comparative analysis of Khoi and Xhosa linguistic relationships shows that their interaction was of long duration. Harinck observes that the Khoi words 'borrowed' by Xhosa are significant from a historian's point of view because they not only provide topographical information, but also point to socio-economic relationships between the two peoples. He singles out the groups of words relating to cattle and religion to show the numerous semantic correspondences of Khoi terms in the Xhosa language.[2] At the same time, he observes that 'the Xhosa retained many Bantu forms for all religious institutions and ritual practices also denoted by Khoi "borrowings", which indicates that these institutions and practices existed prior to contact with Khoi, and were not wholly adopted from Khoi culture'.[3] The study of Xhosa praise-names of the supreme being are of particular interest in this respect.

As we have seen, the terms *uMdali*, *uMenzi*, *uHlanga*, *iNkosi yezulu*, *uMvelingqangi* and *uNkulunkulu* were commonly found among both branches of the Nguni, the Zulu-speaking as well as the Xhosa-speaking people. We have argued, therefore, that these traditional God-names date from before the time the Xhosa broke away from the parent Nguni body and could well be of ancient origin. Comparative evidence from other African societies strengthens this view. On the other hand, in pre-Christian times the Northern Nguni or Zulu-speaking people did not identify with the God-names *Qamata* and *Thixo* (*Tixo*). These terms were clearly adopted by the Xhosa after they branched off and moved into Transkei and Ciskei.

Many Xhosa regard *Qamata* and *Thixo* as designations of

their own,[4] but the implosive consonants or 'clicks' indicate their Khoisan origin. It is not possible to date the time at which these God-names were incorporated into Xhosa religious belief and practice, but the evidence points to *Qamata* predating *Thixo* by a considerable period.

The Xhosa claim that the name *Qamata* is of ancient origin and that *Thixo* only came into common usage during the 19th century. This development in tradition would correspond with their socio-cultural experience. The derivation and meaning of the word *Qamata* is unknown but it could be either of San origin, or else a mixture of Khoi and San as there was a considerable blending of beliefs among these peoples. The uncertainty about the 'borrowing' of this God-name from the Khoisan reflects the speculative nature of the history concerning the interaction between the Xhosa and the Khoisan during the early part of the Xhosa expansion, which could well have extended over a couple of centuries; whereas *Thixo* is unquestionably derived from *Tsui//Goab*, the name of the great national hero of the Khoi, who is generally regarded as their supreme being. A more intensive interaction between the Xhosa and the Khoi during the latter part of the 18th century, together with missionary influence in adopting *Thixo* as the name of the Christian God in the early part of the 19th century, explains why *Thixo* gradually superseded *Qamata* in religious usage among the Xhosa.[5]

A Theoretical Reflection on the Study of Religious Change

As I have already indicated, the incorporation of large numbers of Khoisan individuals into Xhosa society opened the way for cultural diffusion. The question is, though, what influences were at work in determining the selection and acceptance by the Xhosa of particular elements from the Khoisan tradition, more especially the more developed notion of the supreme being.

I have argued elsewhere that words can be 'carriers' of change;[6] and I subscribe to the view that 'religious symbols have the power to shape both culture and society'.[7] In the case of the Xhosa it is evident that the assimilation of the term

Qamata from the incoming culture into their tradition brought with it the concept of a supreme being who was no longer merely a First Cause and Sky Deity, but who was actively involved in human affairs. This can be seen as a profound change in both religious belief and practice.

Cumpsty maintains that the members of a group who have their sense of reality firmly integrated with their socio-cultural experience, will not be open to any serious shift in their understanding of ultimate reality unless their socio-cultural experience has been disturbed.[8] It is my contention that the mixing of the Xhosa with the Khoisan as a result of their movement into Transkei and Ciskei, caused 'cultural migration' which was sufficient to disturb their socio-cultural experience and so create a need to find a new source of power with which to cope with new situations.

The pace of change for the Xhosa was not sufficient to require a radical break with tradition, as was the case when their society disintegrated in the mid-19th century when they were confronted by Christianity and westernization. Rather, new elements were gradually absorbed from the Khoisan culture which served to explain and control their gradually changing situation. The Khoi and the San were both wandering peoples whose religious life focused on a host of supernatural beings; but it was their emphasis on a supreme being who was the ultimate source of power which found favour with the Xhosa.

Cumpsty has emphasized that no symbol will long survive transplantation from one culture to another unless it finds verification in the socio-cultural experience of the receiving tradition.[9] We conclude, therefore, that the symbolic associations of the God-name *Qamata* eventually became absorbed into Xhosa tradition because they 'fitted' the disturbed socio-cultural experience of the Xhosa.

Horton interprets African traditional religion in terms of an 'Intellectualist Theory' which is modelled on the idea of a 'basic' African cosmology which has a two-tiered arrangement of unobservables. In the first tier are the lesser spirits, and they underpin events and processes in the microcosm of the local community and its environment, whilst in the second tier the supreme being underpins events and processes in the macrocosm, i.e. the world as a whole. According to this model, the Khoisan could be expected to have a strong emphasis on the supreme being because their microcosmic boundaries were weak. On the other hand, the religious life of the Xhosa would be concentrated on the lesser spirits, with minimal development of the concept of a supreme being, as long as their social relations remained confined by their microcosmic boundaries.

Horton argues that when change brings about a weakening of the microcosmic boundaries, more attention will be paid to the supreme being because he is seen as underpinning the wider life to which people are moving.[10] 'Migratory drift' can be seen to have made for wider communication which brought about the weakening of the microcosmic boundaries of Xhosa society.[11] And the Xhosa did in fact assimilate new ideas about the supreme being together with certain ritual practices, which made him more approachable. But the change in their way of life was not sufficiently drastic to stimulate the development of a more elaborate system of beliefs and practices associated with a supreme being, and certainly not to move strongly towards transcendence; and the ancestor cult remained the focus of their religious activity. In other words, there was no radical move from what was primarily a behaviour pattern as the principle of cohesion in the community to what was primarily a belief pattern. There was merely a slight shift in emphasis within the behaviour pattern. Further, there continued to be a concern with texture rather than goals in finding a meaning in life, the emphasis being on the quality of life now rather than in the future.

In this type of society man's position vis-à-vis the world is one of relationship, not exploitation. The moral idea is the harmonious integration of the world and the self in it. Life is ordered according to reciprocal obligations and responsibilities, and conformity is at a premium in maintaining harmony. Any sign of individuality is regarded as a breach of custom and as being likely to upset the equilibrium, so endangering the well-being of the community as a whole.

Horton's theory suffers in that western model-making is

being imposed on the existential experience imparting a divided quality. I prefer Wilson's change of scale in which the focus of religion becomes more cosmic as experience broadens;[12] but would emphasize that the religious concern is simply focused at the level of the need, so that in a time of disturbance the overwhelming vitality of the immediate is lost and the entities of the penumbra emphasized. This is represented by Cumpsty's 'Search Stage', transcendence emerging only where the present experience is so disturbed as to be unacceptable.[13]

Qamata: Theories of Origin

The word *Qamata* does not appear in any written sources before the 1870s. At that time both Callaway and Theal commented on the fact 'that it was a name almost universally unknown to white men, and entirely so to white missionaries'.[14] The reason for this, according to the Xhosa, was that the name was too sacred to be used freely, so exhibiting the same sort of reluctance to speak the divine name as the ancient Hebrews.[15] Oral tradition is unanimous in agreeing that it was the name of the supreme being in olden times, before the Xhosa moved into their present country, but its origin has been lost in antiquity. Nkonki gives the tradition of the amaNgqika:

> Long, long ago the Xhosa worshipped *Qamata*. His name was on their tongues. Even during the time of Tshiwo [late 17th century?] and even before then *Qamata* was worshipped by them. They did this before the races arrived who came with *Thixo*.
>
> *Qamata's* name used never to be mentioned in vain. It was sacred because it was the name of the One who was believed to be the Giver of blessings, the Protector, the Receiver of offerings and Giver of luck.
>
> He was a god in heaven. Because of that the sky was a revered place. Never would a finger be pointed at it. If someone wished to point at something in the sky, he did that by means of a bent index finger or fist . . .
>
> The origin of the knowledge of this Supreme Being, like all mythical information, is the ancients. Even with them *Qamata* belonged to the sphere of living which was regarded as being outside the probing intelligence of

man. So too much inquiry about Him was checked by the elderly people.

Qamata used to be the only name for this Supreme Being. The other appellations have been taken from other tribes such as *Nkulunkulu* of the Zulu. *Thixo* was introduced by the missionaries. This popular name for God was taken by the earliest missionaries from the Hottentots (*amaLawu*) . . . After giving the missionaries the term *Thixo*, the Hottentots then acted as interpreters. So this appellation for God was the Xhosa interpretation of the word the Hottentots gave for God.[16]

In traditional Xhosa society it was considered disrespectful even to point a finger at an elderly person, or at an ancestor's grave, let alone at the sky which was the dwelling place of *Qamata*. Recent field research has shown that this taboo concerning *Qamata* is still widely held today.[17]

The origin of the word *Qamata* has been a matter of much speculation. Maingard suggests that it is probably 'the designation of some eponymous hero, with supernatural powers', comparable with *Thixo* alias *Tsui//Goab* of the Khoi.[18] Similarly Kidd surmises that *Qamata* was once either a powerful chief or some semi-supernatural being. He adds that some Xhosa say that he had only one leg, an idea clearly borrowed from the Khoi legend about *Tsui//Goab*.[19] A striking dome-like mountain in the St Mark's district in Transkei is called *eQamata*,[20] and the Rev. H. T. Waters, who founded the Anglican mission there in 1855, says that it was supposed to be named after 'an old Hottentot chief'.[21] Without doubt there is an early association of the name *Qamata* with the Khoisan of that area.

A linguistic analysis must of necessity be speculative. Mabona argues for the Khoi derivation of *Qamata* on the basis of linguistic evidence given by Hahn. The Khoisan group as a whole are said to express the 'ancestor god' as stone, while one Khoi group called the first being by the word for sky (*/homi*), which is interchangeable with the word for stone or mountain (*!homi* or *qhomi*).[22] These terms can be linked with the word *qho-ab*, which denotes a single conical granite hill and is a geological feature of the mid-Angolan highlands and parts of Namibia.[23] Mabona claims that the term *qhomab* would mean 'of stone' and that this is close to the Nguni idea of the god who is beyond the blue stone vault, which is the Nguni conception of the sky.[24] The designation of a conical mountain in Transkei as *eQamata* seems to support this theory.

Another suggestion is that there is a connection between *Qamata* and the Khoi deity mentioned by Buttner in 1716 as *Mathee*, possibly derived from '*ma te*' ('give me').[25] A plausible link can be established too with the San names for the supreme being derived from //*Gaua*, who was conceived both as the ghosts of the dead and as a personified being. The main problem is that the early records of San beliefs on which I have drawn are vague, inconsistent and quite inadequate for a thorough discussion.

Among the Heikum of Etosha Pan, /*Gamab* was spoken of as the creator who received the souls of the dead. He made thunder and lightning, the stars were his fire, and he killed people by means of shooting stars. The San believed that people killed by lightning changed into stars. /*Gamab* was found among the Heikum of north-east Ondonga under the form *Xamaba*. He was conceived of as the supreme being who made all things, including mankind, received the souls of the dead into his home in the sky, and sent rain. He had no wife and no children; and was regarded as benevolent and good, but appeared to have no connection with the moral life of the people. He was prayed to for rain, before and after hunting, before a journey was undertaken, and in case of illness. He could be spoken to by the 'magician' and was thought to inflict illness upon people whom he did not like. The Bergdama had similar ideas about //*Gamab*. The name was said to be derived from //*gama*, water. This was the only supernatural being spoken of by these people and he was regarded as the source of life and death, abundance of food, etc. He was also associated with a sky dwelling to which went the souls of the departed.[26]

Schapera believes that there is a connection between //*Gaua* of the San and //*Gaunab* of the Khoi. In Khoi mythology //*Gaunab* is in conflict with *Tsui*//*Goab*, who is described as their 'rain-god'. Under missionary influence //*Gaunab* assumed the role of the devil as did //*Gamab* among the San, and it is difficult to discover how he was originally conceived. But this may be an example of an original nature deity being both creator and destroyer, which aspects tend to remain in the same deity when the people are under pressure and need to direct malevolence against their enemies and benevolence towards themselves. In a more settled situation these aspects tend to be separated out as experience tends to be harmonious except at its boundaries. Hahn derives //*Gaunab* from //*gau*, meaning to destroy, annihilate. This supernatural being was seen as the cause of sickness and death, was intimately linked with the ghosts of the dead, appeased by sacrificial offerings, and stood in close contact with the 'magicians'.[27]

The connection between //*Gaua* and its various forms among the north-western San, and *Qamata* of the Xhosa, may seem far fetched considering that they lived on opposite sides of the continent; but who knows that this may be evidence of closer contact in earlier ages, or of a similar group living closer to the Xhosa. The Khoi may also have been the connecting link in diffusing ideas. Added to which there is the evidence cited above which suggests a direct link between the word *qhomi* of the Khoi and *Qamata*. Schapera stresses linguistic evidence indicating extensive borrowing of religious ideas between the different Khoi and San groups, as well as between the Khoisan and the Xhosa.

Summing up, it can be said that the name *Qamata* is definitely of Khoisan origin; and considering that the orthographies of the different Khoisan languages were in their infancy when the relevant material was first collected, the linguistic correlations that have been discussed seem significant. Moreover, it has been shown that there is some similarity in the ideas associated with these names.

Xhosa Beliefs concerning *Qamata*

According to information obtained in 1880 from an old Xhosa named Juju, who belonged to the amaNdlambe chiefdom of the amaRharhabe, his people 'considered that *Qamata* was the great spirit, greater even than the spirits of our chiefs, as he, in our opinion, made the chiefs'. Juju added that they 'did not often think about these things'.[28] This supports Theal's findings made a few years earlier when he consulted a group of aged amaNqika, one of whom was 'a celebrated native antiquary'. Theal reported that 'the Kaffirs cannot define their belief concerning *Qamata* very minutely, and they do not trouble themselves with thinking much about the matter'. This, of course, as I have said earlier, is typical of nature religion in a settled situation with its emphasis on the texture of the immediate. In reply to his questioning, these old Xhosa were positive in saying that '*Qamata* was never a man'. He had never been a chief, nor was he the first man, the father of the nations, similar 'to the one the old Fingoes (Mfengu) called *Nkulunkulu*'.[29] But they were extremely vague about his attributes. They could only say that he was greater than all creation, that he was everywhere and was thought to see all things, that he was sometimes asked to help people and was believed to respond, that he was thought to be altogether good though there was some uncertainty about this, and that there was none other like him; 'he is all alone'.[30]

Callaway's Ngqika informant in British Kaffraria was more forthcoming. After affirming that *Ukqamata* (Callaway's spelling) was 'an ancient name' among his people for God, he went on to say:

The Ancients said *Ukqamata* was something perfect, who could do things which men could not do. They spoke as though there was a power above them with the nature of which they were unacquainted. They said nothing about his origin or his mode of being. They did not say he gave them rain; but if there was a drought and the inspired priests (*Amagqirha*)[31] were unable to produce rain, they said, It is *Ukqamata's*, by which they meant to say, that it is his power to cause rain. So if a man was ill, and they had no hope of his recovery, they said, 'It is now in *Ukqamata's* hands'. Or if a man had escaped from danger, they said, '*Ukqamata* saved him'. Or if they were about to make a king, they said, 'May he be elected by *Ukqamata*'.[32]

A number of other sources agree that the name of *Qamata* was involved in times of distress. A man in danger would say, 'O! *Qamata ndincede !* – oh! *Qamata* help me!' and when the danger was over he would attribute his deliverance to the supreme being.[33] When men were going to the chief, they would say, 'It is thine, *Qamata*,' by which they meant: 'We shall have all things managed for us by thee.'[34] Kropf maintains that the praise-name was most commonly used as an expressive utterance, such as '*Sekukokuka – Qamata !*' ('*Qamata* knows!') or '*uQamata makakukangele*' ('May *Qamata* look graciously upon thee!') which is said to a sick person.[35] They also used the name in the form of an exclamation, '*Qamata !*' when taken by surprise, and when sneezing.[36]

For Homer, the sneeze is the most violent form of unpremeditated, uncontrolled bodily action and in that sense has a quality of ecstasy. It suggests vulnerability or a disturbance at the very part where life is most clearly symbolized: in breath, in body fluid, head and chest. The connection between sneezing, the divine and the 'soul' is widespread and very ancient. In Xhosa thought-patterns, frequent sneezing and yawning are regarded as preliminary signs of the ancestors' activities in a person who is being called as a diviner and sneezing during the process of divination is considered a sign that the ancestral spirits are present. Sneezing can also be taken as a blessing.[37]

Information about the nature of *Qamata* was given to Callaway by a Ngqika living near St John's River. According to oral tradition:

> They said *Ukqamata* is a living Spirit (using here not the word *Umoya*, wind, which the missionaries have introduced for Spirit, but *Ukqitela*). They said *Ukqamata* is a living Spirit; but they know not where it dwells; and if asked where it dwells, would answer, 'It goes beside me; and yet I see it not'. And they said, Spirits go out of men to go to *Ukqamata*, to the place where they dwell with him. But, though they said this, they know not where the place is. The corpse does not go to *Ukqamata;* it is the spirit only which goes to him; the corpse remains in the earth.[38]

Callaway was of the opinion that some of these statements were the result of contact with European teachers in some form or other. But, as we have seen, the idea of the souls of the departed being received into the sky-dwelling of the supreme being was a common San belief, and seems an equally likely source of influence considering that the word *ukugqitela*, meaning to pass on, to pass over to,[39] was used and not *umoya*. Traditionally *umoya* was air and wind and was taken over by the missionaries 'as a translation for Biblical concepts of soul, spirit and spirituality in man and of the Holy Spirit'.[40] However, whether the ideas came from San or European, the question is why did they become important to these people at this stage; and maybe this is as a result of the disturbance of their previously settled harmonious life experience. If they are San or Khoi ideas, then almost certainly the disturbance involved was their own geographical and cultural migration; if European, then the disturbance could be the western incursion.

Hirst's findings are that nowadays, diviners (*amagqirha*) talk about *Qamata* as being the wind. He is everywhere. He brings the rain which makes the plants grow, providing sustenance for man and beast. He is said to have brought everything into being, the earth, the ancestors, man, animals and plants. But to him all life is one thing. He does not distinguish between the different forms, hence his remoteness. Because he is so impersonal it is no good going to him to redress your wrongs. The ancestors are different, they are your family and can be manipulated.[41]

NOTES AND REFERENCES

1. C. Ehret, 'Language evidence and Religious History' in Ranger and Kimambo (1972), pp. 45–9.
2. Harinck (1969), pp. 150–1. See also J. A. Louw, *The Nomenclature of Cattle in the South Eastern Bantu Languages* (Communications of Unisa, C 2, 1957).
3. Ibid., p. 152.
4. Callaway (1870), pp. 64–5; J. H. Soga (n.d.), p. 150; Theal (1882), pp. 19–20.
5. Dammann notes that a surprising number of designations for the High God in Africa have been borrowed from foreign languages and gives examples including *uThixo*: *Journal of Religion in Africa* 2: pp. 81–95, 1969.

6. Hodgson (1981), p. 3.
7. Cumpsty (1980), p. 62, who gives the example of the way in which the symbols of Hebrew-Christianity influenced the Graeco-Roman world.
8. Ibid., p. 64.
9. Ibid., p. 62.
10. R. Horton, 'African Conversion', *Africa* 41 (2): pp. 85–108, 1971; and 'On the Rationality of Conversion', *Africa* 45 (3): pp. 219–35, and 45 (4): pp. 373–99, 1975.
11. Elphick (1977), p. 14. n. 27, uses D. Stenning's definition of 'migratory drift' as being 'gradual deviance from traditional transhumance patterns because of competition with other peoples'. 'Migration proper' is defined as 'rapid movement under abnormal circumstances'.
12. G. and M. Wilson, *The Analysis of Social Change* (Cambridge, 1968).
13. I am indebted to Prof. J. S. Cumpsty for this understanding.
14. H. Callaway, 'South African Folk-lore', *Cape Monthly Magazine* n.s. 16: p. 110, 1878; G. M. Theal, 'Sparks from Kafir Anvils', *Cape Monthly Magazine* n.s. 16: p. 191, 1878.
15. Maingard (1934), pp. 135–7. cf. similar taboos among other blacks: McVeigh (1974), p. 61; B. A. Pauw, *Religion in a Tswana Chiefdom* (London, 1960) pp. 31–2; Setiloane (1976), p. 85.
16. Nkonki (1968), pp. 28, 50. See also Theal, *CMM* n.s. 16: p. 192, 1878; and interview with A.M.S. Sityana (praise-poet), Fort Hare, 16 July 1979.
17. E.g. Interviews with Rev. C. C. M. D. Hoyana, East London, 5 August 1978, and A. M. S. Sityana, 16 July 1979. See also Dwane (1979), pp. 10–11, 221.
18. Maingard (1934), p. 135.
19. Kidd (1904), p. 101.
20. 'It is a perfect dome, with a dyke of igneous rock, like the raised ridge of a helmet, passing right over the highest part': McLaren (1940), p. 418. This mountain was visited during research.
21. H. T. Waters, G. 66–'83, *Commission on Native Laws and Customs*, p. 358.
22. T. Hahn, 'The Graves of Heitsi-eibib', *Cape Monthly Magazine* XV1: pp. 259–65, 1873; Hahn (1881), pp. 91, 94. See also Dapper (1668), p. 75 n. 84; Moodie (1840), entry for 5 October 1655. G. S. Nienaber and P. Raper give the meaning of *!homi* or *qhomi* as mountain: *Toponymica Hottentotica* no. 10 (Pretoria, 1980) p. 419.
23. Hahn (1873), p. 259, and (1881), p. 94.
24. Mabona (1973), p. 7 and notes 33 and 34: 'The whole Nguni group believed that the sky was a big revolving vault of blue stone, which harboured numerous inhabitants under the formidable sky chief who wielded thunder and lightning and all the heavenly phenomena.'
25. Nienaber and Raper II (1977), p. 989.
26. This discussion is based on Schapera (1965), pp. 184–5, 188–9, 194–5, 396–7.
27. Ibid., pp. 387–9.
28. 'D', 'Reminiscences of an old Kafir', *Cape Monthly Magazine* 3: p. 294, Nov. 1880.
29. For a discussion on the use of *Nkulunkulu* (*Unkulunkulu*) to denote an origi-

nal ancestor: Berglund (1976), p. 36; Callaway (1870), part 1; Kidd (1904) pp. 96–101; Krige (1936), pp. 280–3.

30. Theal (1882), pp. 19–20; and *CMM* n.s. 16: pp. 191–2, 1878.
31. *amagqirha* – traditional doctors or diviners. In Damara/Nama, the diviner is also called *gqirha*.
32. Callaway, *CMM* 2: pp. 94–5, 1880.
33. Nkonki (1968), p. 28. See also Kidd (1904), p. 101; Kropf and Godfrey (1915), p. 347; Theal, *CMM* n.s. 16: p. 191, 1878.
34. Callaway, *CMM* 2: pp. 93–4, 1880.
35. Kropf and Godfrey (1915), p. 347, and A. Kropf, *Das Volk der Xosa-Kaffern im östlichen Südafrika* (Berlin, 1889); McLaren, (1940), p. 418.
36. Kidd (1904), p. 101.
37. Tyler notes that 'sneezing is regarded by the Zulus as an indication of good health, and immediatly after this operation they ejaculate thanks to the spirits of the ancestors. The exclamation often is: "Spirits of our people, grant me long life!" The time spent in sneezing is considered lucky, for then the spirits are more benevolent than at other times': J. Tyler, *Forty Years Among the Zulus* (Boston and Chicago, 1891) p. 110.
38. Callaway, *CMM* 2: p. 97, 1880.
39. Kropf and Godfrey (1915), p. 128; *–tela*: to pour out into, p. 40.
40. Berglund (1976), p. 85.
41. Interview with M. Hirst, Kaffrarian Museum, King William's Town, 26 May 1981. In his research among the Ndlambe near East London, Bigalke found that it was the 'Red' (traditional) men and women over fifty who knew the name *Qamata*. Younger people referred to *Thixo* and *Mdali*: (1969), p. 70.

7. THE WORSHIP OF *QAMATA*

Ritual Supplication in Times of National Crisis

The problem about evaluating the material on the worship of *Qamata* is that despite the fact that this God-name is associated with a long-standing tradition, the earliest references in the written sources are in the 1870s. In some cases the ritual tradition that has been handed down has clearly been influenced by missionary teaching and practice, even though this may be denied, while the present-day ritual which I recorded, of calling on *Qamata* for rain, purposefully blends traditional and Christian practices so as to appeal to all groups. Nonetheless, although there was no extensive cult of *Qamata*, there is evidence to show that he was approached in times of national crisis such as war, drought and epidemic disease of men and their animals.

Those at the top of the social order were thought to be closest to *Qamata* and so it was the chief, councillors, elders and, more rarely the homestead head, who were the mediators. Juju, whose father Pantsi had been circumcized the same year as Rharhabe, was one of this Xhosa chief's councillors and had crossed over the Kei River with him some time around 1770, relates the following tradition:

> In times of great national trouble we were called together
> by our chiefs to intercede with *Qamata*. The order
> observed on these occasions was as follows: When all the
> principal men of the tribe had at the chief's bidding
> assembled at the Great Place, a ring would be formed of
> the men all sitting in silence with their faces to the ground.
> Then one of the youngest councillors would rise, and
> looking upwards as the Christians do, call upon *Qamata*
> to help them in their time of distress. When he had
> finished his petition, another councillor – an older man –
> would speak some time to *Qamata* in the same strain,
> and the chief would follow, and when he had done
> speaking or praying the meeting would disperse. There
> was no killing at such gatherings, and with the exception
> of the three principal actors no one spoke.[1]

Qamata: Rain and the Rainmaker

It is not my intention to provide an overview of the whole range of Xhosa religious beliefs and practices; but in looking at the role of *Qamata* in bringing about rain, it is first necessary to give some consideration to rainmaking ceremonies on their own terms.[2] Traditionally a number of different reasons were given for why the sky withheld rain. One belief was that it was a manifestation of the ancestors' displeasure. Another popular notion was that the rain could be delayed by the evil influences of witchcraft and sorcery, and the person supposedly responsible had to be identified by the 'rain-doctors' and generally was put to death. So for example, during the great drought of 1800, Nontsangani was 'smelled out for scaring off the rain'. Witches are often pictured as behaving in ways that directly reverse the normal. Nontsangani was accused of causing the drought 'by the indecency of walking about naked . . . (and) by her walking on her hands, the soles of her feet turned towards the sky'.[3]

When the rains failed rainmakers were summoned and, as Peires observes, 'the odd showers which occasionally attended their ceremonies brought psychological as well material relief'.[4] He further comments that during periods of prolonged drought it was the chiefdom as a whole which acted. It was the chief's responsibility to bring the rain and it was he who raised a levy of cattle to pay a celebrated rainmaker.[5] Over the years the Xhosa patronized rainmakers from all the different groups with which they came into contact, Khoi, San and Mfengu, and the missionaries were approached too in the hope that they would be effective in tapping a superior power. Van der Kemp records that during the drought of 1800, after the rainmaker had failed, he was put under considerable pressure by Ngqika to pray to his God for rain. He was greatly blessed when heavy rain fell shortly after he had prayed. A Xhosa subsequently commented: 'Tinkhanna (Nyengana alias Van der Kemp) has talked to the Lord on high; and he has given us rain.'[6]

There are a number of vivid descriptions of Xhosa rainmaking ceremonies in the early written sources which tally in essential details.[7] In the account given by Shaw (1860), the rainmaker Gqindiva was asked for rain by the chief Phato because the country was 'dead with drought'.[8] On this occasion the missionary was held responsible for keeping back the rain as the ringing of the mission bell at Wesleyville was said to drive the rain clouds away. Shaw countered by laying the blame on the rainmaker, reasoning that it was because people approached him instead of God.

Two points are significant in the account which Shaw gives of his dispute with the rainmaker: that Gqindiva claimed not to make the rain but to 'seek' it; and that he agreed with the missionary that God gives the rain (much to Shaw's scorn), yet he asked 'rain from the spirits'.[9] This can be linked with the notions about *Qamata* in relation to rain recorded by Callaway in 1875, from a Ngqika informant in British Kaffraria: 'They did not say he (*Qamata*) gave the rain; but if there was a drought and the inspired priests (*amagqirha*) were unable to produce rain, they said, "It is *Ukqamata's*", by which they meant to say, that it is his power to cause rain.'[10]

Despite the fact that *Qamata* was conceived as having 'the power to cause rain', he was not generally personified in the natural elements. But Xhosa poets such as Jolobe have referred to a thunderstorm as a manifestation of *Qamata's* wrath resulting from certain transgressions of law and custom. Significantly one specific transgression was Ngqika's abduction of his uncle Ndlambe's wife, Thuthula.[11] In Xhosa law this was an incestuous relationship and a grave violation of custom by the chief. Such was the fear of Ngqika's followers that they would all suffer some sort of supernatural retribution, that they deserted to Ndlambe in large numbers.[12]

Calling on Qamata for Rain

One source mentions that in times of drought the people used to visit the graves of the Xhosa chiefs in order to appeal to them to ask *Qamata* to send rain.[13] The more usual practice was for a chief and his people to ascend a high hill or mountain to supplicate *Qamata* for rain. The ritual is not described in the historical records but the many references in Xhosa literature, together with reports of similar communal rituals among the Thembu and Zulu, support oral evidence that this

77

custom was an old Xhosa tradition. The ritual is still widely practised by Xhosa today in times of severe drought, with the Christians adding new associations and practices to it.[14]

Fawcett notes that in classical mythology, 'the mountain represented symbolically the point at which the divine and the human met together'.[15] It was therefore natural to speak of the top of the mountain as the dwelling place of the gods; but mythological man only periodically ascended into the mountain to meet his God. This of course would only be true of a sky god where the need for a symbol of transcendence had not yet emerged.

As I have tried to show, the absence of early written material about *Qamata* is because the missionaries were not aware of this concept of the supreme being before the 1870s; but the evidence indicates that it was a well established tradition among the Xhosa by the 19th century. Similarly I suggest that the absence of any account of the ritual intercession of *Qamata* for rain in contemporary mission records is because no missionary was ever privileged to witness this most sacred ritual. It is important to remember that it only took place when the efforts of the rainmakers had failed and the drought had reached critical proportions. This might not be for a decade at a time. An account of the ritual as practised in Ciskei has been set down from the oral tradition by Raum and De Jager and purports to relate to pre-Christian times:

> The chief would tell his people to brew beer, which was then taken to the great place and from there to a hill. Everyone would be dressed in traditional attire, and they would dance (*batshile*) and call in chorus: *Sicela imvula, Qamata.* ('We're asking for rain, *Qamata.*') The clouds would then gather and rain fall profusely until the rivers overflowed, making it difficult for the people to return to their homes. They would withdraw to the great place and drink, eat, and dance there until the rivers subsided.[16]

Another source maintains that they had to refrain from intercourse, i.e., be ritually pure, before going up the mountain to approach *Qamata.*[17] In its Christianized form a minister can lead the ritual and in a newspaper report of a service held on a hill-top in Transkei, Pauw observes that 'the preacher's text, *Uyakufumana ukuphila* (you will be healed) reflects a concern with the sustenance of life in general, not with rain and crops alone'.[18] However, when information was collected on a visit to Ciskei in February 1980 during a severe drought, similar services were being held throughout the area specifically to pray for rain.

Traditionally the chief is the mediator; and information was obtained from Chief S. M. Burns-Ncamashe as to the way in which he leads the service on the hill-top behind his home at KwaGwali.[19] His people are a mixed group and the ritual is drawn from both the Christian and Xhosa traditions; but basically 'the idea is to go up the mountain in order to meet God at a special place to pray for rain', and this is rooted in pre-Christian Xhosa tradition.

Each area is said to have a special place and at KwaGwali it is an outcrop of rocks on the hill-top. The chief wears his traditional regalia of karosses, while many of the men wear blankets, and the women, traditional skirts. The ritual begins at the cattle byre, 'the seat of the ancestral spirits', so that the ancestors can be summoned to accompany them to the place of worship in the traditional way. All the elderly men enter the byre and the chief then addresses the ancestors. Following this the chief and his elders proceed to the top of the hill. The women and children go ahead and sing church hymns and traditional songs while they wait. There is more singing during the service, including Ntsikana's 'Great hymn' (*'Ulo Thixo omkhulu'*), as well as prayers, an address by the chief to state the purpose of their being there, and possibly also a Bible reading. The passage favoured is from I Kings 18 where Elijah has a contest with the prophets of Baal on Mount Carmel and brings the drought to an end with his ritual, showing that Yahweh has the power to control rain and fertility.

The Xhosa practice of invoking *Qamata* for rain seems to draw heavily on Khoisan belief and practice. The supreme beings of both the Khoi and the San were regarded as rain-givers and were prayed to for rain. The annual rainmaking ceremony of the Khoi was their most important religious ceremony and was rich in symbolic ritual. It was aimed 'directly at providing an adequate supply of rain for the life of the tribe'.[20]

Laubscher describes a communal ritual which appears similar to the Xhosa one and which was traditionally practised by the Thembu when they wished to approach *uMdali* for help during periods of prolonged drought or epidemics of sickness among humans and animals. It took place on the summit of a hill or mountain, and songs were interspersed with prayers to *uMdali*.[21] This ritual was called *umtendeleko*, the name of a traditional family or social feast held on any special occasion. The word was adopted by missionaries to designate the Lord's Supper.[22]

Berglund describes a comparable ritual which the Zulu carry out when they wish to call on the Lord-of-the-Sky in times of urgent need. He emphasizes that it must be done in an orderly fashion and that appropriate preparations must be made before approaching the supreme being.[23] According to him, the ritual intercession takes place on certain characteristic hills and mountains scattered around in Natal and Zululand, on which nobody builds and where cattle are preferably not grazed. A photograph of one such mountain shows that it is conical and very similar in appearance to *eQamata* in Transkei. On the summit of these high places is found an *isiguqo*, a kneeling place, which can be marked with a circle of stones.

Nowadays the ritual is carried out by Christians and Zionists as well as traditionalists, and a day is appointed by the different leaders for their people to mount the hill to pray for rain. At the summit they approach the *isiguqo* with great reverence, crawling forward on hands and knees and remaining kneeling while their leader makes their supplications known to the Lord-of-the-Sky. Eloquence of language and dignified behaviour are said to be prerequisites for the prayer-leader. Again Christian influences have changed the content of the service but the tradition appears to be long established.

Supportive historical evidence comes from Tyler (1891), who spent 40 years as a missionary in Zululand. He records that no Zulu dared point a finger at these special hills or mountains, 'lest thunder and hail storms result'.[24] The clenched fist was used instead, as when pointing to the sky, and this custom prevails to this day.[25] The indications are that the practice of calling on the supreme being for rain pre-dated Xhosa and Khoisan interaction, the difference being the identification of the supreme being as *Qamata*.

Rainmaking and Driving off Storms

Recent research has shown that *Qamata* may be invoked in rainmaking rituals and in driving off storms. It is impossible to date these traditions and there may well be missionary influence here. However, they may equally well be old customs as they 'fit' the thought-patterns about *Qamata* and early records of the Khoi report a similar symbolic rainmaking ritual.[26] Berglund reports comparable traditional rituals among the Zulu in relation to the Lord-of-the-Sky too.[27] Mbiti's findings in other African societies are that 'on the whole (rainmakers) exercise their profession in consultation with God', but of course God is more significant in some of these societies than in others.[28]

The rainmaker, *igogo* or *igqirha lemvula*, described by Malan is said to have the exclusive function of approaching *Qamata* for rain.[29] The rainmaker mixes his herbs and medicines in a baked clay pot, *ingqayi*. The mixture is stirred with a special forked stick, *ixhayi*, which symbolizes lightning. The stick is rubbed gently in the palms of the hands until the contents of the pot foam. This is supposed to represent clouds. During the whole ceremony the rainmaker talks constantly to *Qamata*, asking him to bring rain. If the rain does not come, the failure is ascribed to transgressions against the ancestors and they must be placated with a ritual killing. The sacrifice is also thought to rouse the goodwill of *Qamata*. Afterwards the rainmaking ceremony is repeated.

The thought-world underlying this ritual shows that *Qamata* is regarded as determining the course of nature, so that it is he who must be approached when disasters are caused by natural forces. In all other cases such as sickness, misfortune or death, it is the ancestral spirits who are approached. The supreme being is also said to be concerned with the right relationship between men and their ancestral spirits, because when these relationships are seriously disturbed he will inflict natural disasters on the people until harmony is restored. For this reason the rainmaker urges the people to make sacrifices to their ancestors when *Qamata* holds back the rain.

Malan also describes a ritual procedure followed to deflect impending thunderstorms or hurricanes, which is associated with the supreme being. A woman who has borne twins is sought because it is believed that she has been blessed by *Qamata* in a particular way and that the threatening storm will listen to her commands. She takes the cloth or skin in which the twins are usually wrapped and waves it in the direction of the storm, saying repeatedly: *'Yiya emaMpondweni !'* ('Go to Mpondoland!') When the storm changes course, doing no damage to the cattle or crops, *Qamata* is thought to have responded to the people's request through the woman's mediation.[30]

A Ritual Killing to Propitiate *Qamata*

It is clear that prayer was the main element in ritual practices relating to *Qamata*. Beer and dancing were sometimes included but no mention is made of a ritual killing, unlike the propitiation to *iNkosi yezulu* after death by lightning, sacrifices generally being reserved for the ancestors. Callaway was told by a Zulu informant that there had once been *izibongo* or praise-names with which to praise *Unkulunkulu*, but these had been lost in the course of time because he no longer had a son who could worship him. The ancestors could be worshipped because their *izibongo* were known by their descendants, but there were no names to worship *Unkulunkulu*.[31]

At the *idini* or ritual killing which is made to propitiate an ancestral spirit who has been divined as causing sickness, the recitation of the clan names of the sufferer, interspersed with certain verbal formulae, *ukunqula*, is a ritual invocation of the spirits. According to Hammond-Tooke, this is the only killing at which there is prayer and provides proof that the ancestors are worshipped.[32]

Strangely enough it is Callaway who gives the only example of a ritual killing directed to *Qamata* in former times. The

Ngqika whom he interviewed at St John's River in the 1870s, told him that the name of *Qamata* existed among the first amaRharhabe and was not taken from any other people. He confirmed the statements of Callaway's other Ngqika infcr-mants concerning the nature of *Qamata*, and then went on to say:

> If a man was ill, they killed a bullock and called on *Ukqamata*, that he might raise him up from his sickness; when the bullock was killed an old man stood forth and prayed thus, *'Kqamata*, look upon thy son, and raise him up from his sickness'. And before eating the flesh of the sacrifice a piece called *UmKhotsho*, or *Ukqamata's* portion was set aside, and when all the rest was eaten, they ate that also.[33]

Prayer and *Izivivane*

The St John's River informant also told Callaway that just as they had taken over *Thixo* for God instead of *Qamata* from the Hottentots, so they had taken *ukuthandaza* to pray, instead of *ukukusa*, and prayed thus to *Qamata*: 'Oh mayst thou be pleased to regard us at all times when enemies shall beset us.' Kropf says that *ukuthandaza* originally meant to pray for mercy or life, but later came to be used for prayer in general.[34] He gives the meaning of *ukukusa* as to screen from (wind or rain), to shelter; with the figurative meaning of to protect from violence, to keep safe.[35] It is possible that Callaway meant *ukukuza* as one of its meanings is to praise and this seems a more likely connection.[36] Callaway thought that if *Qamata* was found to be the name of an ancestor, in accordance with the religious legends of other tribes, it had 'evidently been stripped of its anthropomorphism'.[37]

A form of prayer apparently borrowed from the Khoi was associated with the *izivivane* or heaps of stones found at road-sides, near river fords and on mountain tops. There are numerous theories about the origin of these cairns but the Khoi regarded them as graves connected with *Heitsi Eibib*, who was either a legendary hero or a mythical ancestor. The practice was to add stones, branches and other objects to the cairns while praying to *Heitsi Eibib* for success in hunting, plentiful cattle and other material benefits.[38] This custom was also re-ported for the San.[39]

Izivivane were found throughout Xhosa country and the practice of the Khoi was followed by the Xhosa. A passer-by would pick up a stone, green branch or bunch of grass, spit on it, and then throw it onto the cairn. Sometimes this was done without a word, other times a simple prayer was said which could include a plea for strength and health, an abundant supply of food on the way, and good luck in accompanying the journey's purpose. This practice is widely documented by early travellers in Kaffraria, but they could find no tradition as to how the cairns had originated and all the Xhosa could say was that it was the custom of their ancestors.[40] They had a superstitious dread that neglect of the ritual would lead to misfortune. Xhosa tradition claims that Rharhabe encouraged 'the form of worship associated with *izivivane* and disseminated it among the people',[41] but the Xhosa prayers were never as elaborate as those of the Khoi.[42]

Some Xhosa say that the prayer was made to the cairn itself: '*Sivivane ndiphe amandla*' ('*Sivivane* give me strength'). But most relate that it was the supreme being who was invoked, the earlier records using *Qamata*, the later ones *Thixo: 'Qamata ndincede*' ('God help me'). The ancestors could also be in-cluded: 'May God and the spirits of my fathers befriend me in the hour of need.'[43] Kropf says that no matter whether the object of the journey was good or evil, whether the traveller was going to steal his neighbour's cattle, or to pay a visit to his friends, or to pay his addresses to a young woman, he would use the same form.[44] The cairns were found scattered throughout Mpondo[45] and Zulu[46] country too, and the same ritual was practised. (A similar custom is said to exist in other parts of Africa as well as in Europe, North America, New Zealand, Borneo, Polynesia and Central Asia,[47] and of course in the Biblical tradition.)[48]

Bryant argues against the *izivivane* being graves in the Zulu area for the following reasons. Firstly, that the Zulu had no tradition whatever that they were graves. Secondly, when they threw stones, they made no appeal to any spirits but only spat on them. Thirdly, the Zulu never had the custom of burying anybody alongside the public highways, where the *izivivane* were always found. And fourthly, the heaps were frequently found on rocky or stony ground where it would be impossible to dig a grave. He concludes that they were 'merely superstitious "luck-heaps" '.[49] Berglund contends that they were a traditional road-sign and that spitting on the stone was a symbol of innocence.[50]

On the surface the ritual appears to have a purely magical purpose; but the fact that *Qamata* was invoked suggests a deeper religious significance for some at least. Just as the ancestral spirits were associated with the homestead and its immediate environs, and had their sacred places there, so was the supreme being associated with the wider universe of nature beyond the spirits' protection, and the cairns could have symbolized a point of contact with *Qamata*, as did the high places. The ritual invocation while throwing a stone can be seen as a momentary communion with *Qamata*, a supreme being who became more approachable under Khoi influence. Certainly *izivivane* seem to have the connotation of a localized divine presence such as one might associate in Catholic practice with the altar; if not *Qamata* then the ancestral spirits. The blowing out of water in a ritual context symbolizes purity, for if there is anger in a person's heart the ritual may be ineffective.[51]

Qamata and the Ancestors

There is a strong tradition that *Qamata* was approached through the ancestors. The Xhosa world-view holds that there is an hierarchical ordering of life in this world and the next, and it is claimed that the ancestral spirits have always acted as mediators between man, who stood at the bottom, and *Qamata*, who stood at the top.[52] This imagery is modelled on social and political life, and is said to be a wide-spread notion among other Bantu-speaking peoples.[53] Opinion is divided as to whether it is a modern innovation inspired by missionary teaching, or not; but, as field research has shown, it is a popular belief among Xhosa today. This is how the veneration of the ancestors is reconciled with Christianity, although the radical separation between this place and the place of *Qamata*, which would be appropriate in what Cumpsty terms 'Religion of Secular World Affirmation' (Christianity) in his typology, would hardly have been part of the original concept.

The intercessory role of the ancestors is rationalized by the Xhosa in a number of ways. First, there is the idea that the ancestral spirits dwell in the same spiritual realm as *Qamata* and are therefore in a better position to approach him than man.[54] At the same time, the ancestors are part of the extended family and because they know the needs of their descendants on earth they are effective go-betweens. Linked to this is the idea 'that just as any person who is a new arrival in a new environment may approach local authority through the mediation of one of the well-known residents, so also the living who are not familiar with God, ask the ancestral spirits who are closer to him to intercede on their behalf'.[55] Another notion is based on the cardinal values of reverence and respect for seniority and status. In the same way that it would be considered a dishonour and irreverence for a child to mention his father's name, so it would be an act of dishonour and irreverence to communicate either by prayer or by sign with the supreme being.[56] Similarly, a chief is never approached directly. Reverence and respect for the chief are shown by going through a mediator, his councillors fulfilling this role.[57] Nor does the chief speak to his subjects directly but rather through a spokesman.[58] *Qamata* is the *Inkosi Enkulu* (the Great Chief) and no mortal would have the audacity to speak to him directly.[59] One tradition says that if you did communicate directly with the supreme being you would be killed by lightning, and if you ever saw him you would cease to be.[60]

This reluctance to address the great deity should not be confused with transcendence in the sense in which we have been using that word. This is not a radical gap but simply the principle of keeping the background undefined which we find in Canaanite religion, where *El* was in the background and technically the supreme figure in the pantheon, but *Ba'al* received the worship. This principle is also found in Zoroastrianism, where *Zerran*, the old fire god, was at some stage resurrected to serve this purpose when *Ahura Mazdah* became too clearly defined. Even in the Religion of Secular World Affirmation, which is perhaps where Zoroastrianism belongs, a *deus absconditus* is a necessary corollary to the limitations of language.

Burns-Ncamashe illustrates the mediatorial function of the ancestors in his account of a traditional form of 'speaking-out' in private.

> If a person felt a deep sense of guilt and did not feel moved to make a public confession, he would go to the forest and look for a deep hole. There he would kneel and pour out all his wrongdoing. Whenever people heard this, the women as they were gathering wood, the men as they were hunting, they would listen and from the words that were said they would move quietly away so as not to disturb the person making his confession. They knew what was happening because it was the common practice.
>
> The idea of using the hole was because the bones of the ancestors, the chiefs, the great men of the country, were in the earth and their spirits were supposed to be somewhere there too. The spirits of the departed were supposed to hear the confession and were going to convey this to the greatest of all spirits who would then somehow give absolution. But it would not be pronounced so that it could be heard. It would be seen in the change, the worry would go and there would be more luck and good fortune. Then the person felt absolved.[61]

The practice of 'speaking-out' into the hole could be very old, the need to restore harmony with the ancestors being vital; but the confession-absolution language appears to manifest Christian influence.[62] Despite the strenuous efforts to defend the idea of the intercessory role of the ancestors by Christian blacks, as given in the evidence above, I agree with Hammond-Tooke that there is nothing in indigenous concepts to indicate that the ancestors mediate between the supreme being and man; and that such an idea is almost certainly due to missionary influence.[63] As Peires argues too, there is no reason why there should have been a coherent relationship between the ancestors and the supreme being because they operated on totally distinct planes.[64] One of the ways in which religious change has taken place as African societies expanded in scale, has been the casting of the ancestors in new roles and the linking of them to new causes in order for them to meet new needs in new situations.[65]

NOTES AND REFERENCES

1. 'Reminiscences of an old Kaffir,' *CMM* 3: pp. 293–4, 1880. For a general discussion on intermediaries in the worship of God in African societies: Mbiti (1970), ch. 19.
2. I am indebted to Dr J. Peires for bringing this point to my notice: Communication, 1 January 1982.
3. N. Falati, 'The Story of Ntsikana. A Gaika Xhosa' (translated by C. Falati and C. Mpaki, St Mark's, 1895 – MS, Cory Library, Rhodes University) p. 1. Falati goes on to describe the manner of her death, pinioned on a red-hot rock to bake in the sun.
4. Peires (1981), p. 8.
5. Ibid., pp. 33, 64. See also J. H. Soga (n.d.), p. 175.
6. Entries for 30 October and 2 November, Van der Kemp's Journal: *Transactions* I, p. 427.
7. E.g. Alberti (1810), p. 52; Backhouse (1844), p. 278; Lichtenstein (1812–15) I: pp. 316–7.
8. Shaw (1860), pp. 460–6.
9. Ibid., pp. 462–3. Holden (1866), pp. 309–11, gives a comparable account of a dispute between Livingstone and a Bechuana rainmaker.
10. Callaway, *CMM* 2: pp. 94–5, 1880.
11. J. J. R. Jolobe, 'Thuthula', quoted in Dwane (1979), p. 45.
12. Warner's notes in Maclean (1866), p. 62; J. H. Soga (n.d.), p. 62.
13. The place mentioned is Mncotsho near Berlin, a small town between East London and King William's Town: Dwane (1979), p. 18. For burial places of chiefs see F. Brownlee, *African Affairs* 43: pp. 23–4, 1944.
14. Pauw (1975), p. 63.
15. Fawcett (1970), pp. 122–3.
16. O. F. Raum and E. J. de Jager, *Transition and Change in a Rural Community* (Fort Hare, 1972), p. 191.
17. Interview with Fr A. Fischer, McKays Nek Mission, Transkei, 5 August 1981.
18. *Imvo Zabantsundu*, 15 February 1964, quoted in Pauw (1975), p. 81. Fr Fischer suggests that the text should be translated as 'you will be healthy'.
19. Interview with Chief S. M. Burns-Ncamashe, KwaGwali, 18 February 1980. The chief is a leading member of the Order of Ethiopia.
20. Schapera (1965), pp. 378–83.
21. B. J. F. Laubscher, *Sex, Custom and Psychopathology* (London, 1937), pp. 106–9.
22. Kropf and Godfrey (1915), p. 408. See also Davis (1872), p. 212; Döhne (1857), p. 412.

23. Berglund (1976), pp. 44–6.
24. Tyler (1891), p. 111.
25. Berglund (1976), p. 44.
26. Schapera (1965), pp. 378–80.
27. Berglund (1976), pp. 46–63.
28. Mbiti (1970), p. 225.
29. J. S. Malan, 'Die tradisionele Religie van die Xhosa' (unpublished M.A. thesis, Randse Afrikaanse Universiteit, 1968), pp. 15–7. See also T. B. Soga, *Intlalo ka Xhosa* (Lovedale, 1936), p. 92. J. H. Soga gives a very prejudiced account of the Xhosa rainmaker, and makes no mention of *Qamata:* (n.d.), pp. 175–7.
30. Malan (1968), p. 14.
31. Callaway (1870), p. 18.
32. W. D. Hammond-Tooke, 'Do the South Eastern Bantu Worship their Ancestors?' in *Social System and Tradition in Southern Africa*, edited by J. Argyle and E. Preston-Whyte (Cape Town, 1978), pp. 144–6.
33. Callaway, *CMM* 2: p. 96, 1880. Raum and de Jager report that nowadays homesteads can be dedicated to *Qamata* or the ancestors. In this dedication, *ukwazisa*, the offering is a slaughtered goat and brewed beer: (1972), p. 185.
34. Kropf and Godfrey (1915), p. 404. Döhne believes it to be a figurative meaning taken from the custom of turning round or bending over during prayer: (1857), p. 338.
35. Ibid., p. 202.
36. Ibid., p. 204.
37. Callaway, *CMM* 2: p. 98, 1880.
38. For a discussion on the tradition of *Heitsi Eibib:* D. R. Bengston, 'Three African Religious Founders', *Journal of Religion in Africa* VII (fasc. 1): 16–26; Schapera (1965), pp. 373–4, 383–6. See also C. R. Thunberg, *Travels in Europe, Africa and Asia made between the years 1770 and 1779* II (2nd ed., London, 1975), p. 96.
39. Stow (1905), p. 127.
40. E.g. Backhouse (1844), p. 231; Kay (1833), pp. 211–2; Lichtenstein I (1812–15), p. 313; Rose (1829), p. 147; A. Sparrman, *A Voyage to the Cape of Good Hope, 1772–6* II (Dublin, 1785), pp. 201–3.
41. Nkonki (1968), p. 50.
42. In the Khoi prayers *Heitsi Eibib* is addressed as 'our Grandfather' and is asked for luck in hunting and success in finding honey and roots: Hahn (1881), p. 69.
43. Bokwe (1914), p. 3; Cook (n.d.), p. 96; McLaren (1940), p. 424 (he adds that the stone was sometimes wrapped in a piece of cloth); Theal (1882), p. 20.
44. Kropf and Godfrey (1915), p. 454.
45. Hunter records a lengthier prayer among the Mpondo: 'Look upon me God (*Thixo*) of our people. I ask strength of you, you God who created us in the earth. Look upon us. Give us to eat.' (1961), p. 270.
46. A. T. Bryant, *The Zulu People* (Pietermaritzburg, 1949), p. 732; Vilakazi (1948), p. 836; Jenkinson (1882), p. 33; Leslie (1875), p. 146.

47. Bryant (1905), p. 682; Callaway (1870), pp. 66–7; Kidd (1904), pp. 263–7; Willoughby (1932), pp. 20–33. For a general discussion on *izivivane* in Southern Africa see N. J. van Warmelo, 'A Tale of a Heap of Stones', *Africana Notes and News* 16: pp. 278–83, 1964–5.

48. E.g. Genesis 31:46, 48, 52.

49. Bryant (1949), p. 732.

50. Berglund (1976), pp. 334–5.

51. Wilson (1971), p. 65.

52. Dwane (1979), pp. 17–21. For a general discussion on the hierarchy of forces see P. Tempels, *Bantu Philosophy* (Paris, 1969).

53. Nürnberger (1975), p. 187; Mbiti (1970), pp. 230–3; Pauw (1960), p. 31.

54. Dwane (1979), p. 20; J. H. Soga (n.d.), p. 150.

55. S. J. Wallis (ed.), *Inkolo Namasiko aBantu* (London, 1930), p. 1.

56. 'Some Native Beliefs,' *Zonnebloem College Magazine* 3(12): p. 10, Easter 1905.

57. Interview with Chief S. M. Burns-Ncamashe, KwaGwali, 25 October 1978.

58. For a full discussion on the traditional status of a chief see Peires (1981), pp. 27–42.

59. Dwane (1979), p. 221.

60. Interview with Prof Z. S. Qangule and B. Somhlahlo, Fort Hare, 25 October 1978.

61. Interview with Chief S. M. Burns-Ncamashe (Xhosa historian, author, poet), KwaGwali, 25 October 1978.

62. Dwane's discussion on the understanding of sin in the Xhosa tradition seems to show signs of Christian influence too: (1979), pp. 42–6.

63. Hammond-Tooke in Argyle and Preston-Whyte (1978), p. 138.

64. Peires, communication, 1 January 1982.

65. Wilson indicates some of the causes to which the ancestors have been linked in recent times: (1971), pp. 41–2.

8. KHOI AND MISSIONARY INFLUENCE ON XHOSA BELIEFS *UTHIXO* AND *UMTYHOLI*

The Origin of the God-named *Thixo*

The origin of the word *Thixo* is well documented as being derived from *Tsui//Goab* (*Tsuni-//Goam*), the great hero of the Khoi from whom they are said to have taken their origin.[1] The name was written down by early travellers and missionaries in a multitude of different forms and also appears as *Tiqua, Tuiqua, Tuiqoa, Tigoa, Tanquoa, Thuickwe, Thuuikwe, Tsoi Koap, Tsoeikoap, Tshu'Koab, Tsu-goam*, etc. The meaning of the name is usually given as 'sore or wounded knee'. According to Khoi myth, *Tsui//Goab* was a great chief and warrior who went to war with another chief, *//Gaunab*, because the latter was always killing great numbers of his people. They had numerous battles until *Tsui//Goab* became strong enough to kill *//Gaunab*. However, his enemy managed to give him a blow on the knee before expiring, and henceforth he was lame. As the conqueror he became deified by later generations. He was reputed to have had extraordinary powers during his lifetime; and besides being a renowned warrior of great strength, he was said to be a powerful magician and a seer. Legend credits him with coming to life several times after dying. He ultimately came to be regarded as the personification of the natural forces producing rain.[2]

The Khoi worshipped *Tsui//Goab* as the benevolent being who gave them rain, provided them with food and was responsible for their good health; and as the avenger who protected them from all evil. He was ubiquitous and the people took oaths by him, which is said to signify that he was regarded as a moral being who averted evil. When taken by surprise they would use his name as an exclamation: *'Tsui-//Goatse!'* He was invoked at dawn each day with the face turned towards the east. The public prayers were said to have been expressed in poetic form and were often sung as hymns. As with the Xhosa sky-god, *Tsui//Goab* was identified with thunder and lightning. When a thunderstorm was approaching, the people would assemble for a ritual dance and sing a hymn invoking the thunder to leave them alone as they were 'guiltless'. If it thundered, the people would say that it was *Tsui//Goab* speaking and that he was scolding them.[3]

The most important festival was the rain-making ceremony which was held about November or December each year, when the old men judged that the summer rains were due. This was the occasion for the coming together of all the chief's people, so establishing some sort of social cohesion. The religious ritual at the ceremony was rich in symbolism and included the sacrificial killing of animals, a great tribal dance and communal prayers in which *Tsui//Goab* was invoked for plentiful rain and food.[4] The return of the Pleiades each year was another occasion for such prayers. It is clear that the Khoi regarded *Tsui//Goab* as the ultimate source of all power as well as the great ancestor, and that they worshipped him as the supreme being.[5] But even though, in Horton's terms, the microcosmic boundaries of the Khoi were weak, and, as could be expected, the supreme being loomed large in their life in addition to the considerable attention which they gave to lesser spirits,[6] their world-view remained monistic, being pervaded by the divine, and there was no radical gap between man and the supreme being.

Khoi and Missionary Influence

When Van der Kemp first set foot among the Xhosa in 1799, he reported that they had 'no word to express Deity by', and that the king, Ngqika, and his followers therefore used the Hottentot name *Tuikwa*.[7] A couple of months later he again mentioned the fact that this God-name had been 'borrowed from the Hottentots'.[8] In his account of Xhosa religion which he wrote after spending 18 months among the Xhosa, he concluded that 'if by religion we understand reverence for God, or the external action by which that reverence is expressed: I never could perceive that they had any religion, nor any idea of the existence of a God.'[9] He then went on to say that he was of course 'speaking nationally', for there were many individuals who had some notion of God's existence, 'which they had received from adjacent nations'; and that these individuals called the deity *Thiko*, which was 'a corruption of *Thuike*, the name by which God is called in the language of the Hottentots'.[10]

Van der Kemp's reliance on a Khoi interpreter, together with the antagonism of Ngqika and his followers, was hardly conducive to a penetrating insight into Xhosa religion. Nonetheless, I suggest that his observations show that the Xhosa were not merely using *Thixo* to refer to the Khoi God; but that many of those in the frontier district, who had mixed with the Khoi, were either in the process of adopting, or had already adopted, the *Thixo* concept for themselves. This is supported by Bleek's findings as to how the word *Tsui//Goab* was diffused among different people by migrating Khoi, taking on different forms.[11] Furthermore, one strand of the Xhosa tradition holds that *Thixo* 'was introduced [to the Xhosa] when they came into contact with the Hottentots'.[12]

The first converts to Christianity were mostly Gonaqua Khoi or Gqunukhwebe, a mixture of Gonaqua and Xhosa, and as they were the first interpreters to the missionaries the name *Thixo* was perpetuated in expressing the Christian concept of God. Although the missionaries agreed on the Khoi derivation of *Thixo*, their differences in opinion as to its original meaning were as many and varied as was their spelling of the word: *uThixo, uTikxo, uTixo, Thiko, Utika, Utikla, Utikwa, Tuikwa, Thuuicke*, etc. Van der Kemp believed that the word signified 'one who induces pain'.[13] This is possibly a misunderstanding of the derivation of the name *Tsui//Goab* (*tsu* meaning sore), or else it arose from the idea of *Thixo* manifesting his wrath in thunder and lightning. Brownlee (in the 1820s) was of the opinion that it was the Hottentot word for beautiful,[14] while Ayliff said that it should be pronounced *Utikwa*, the literal meaning of which was 'my arm or strength'.[15] This lack of understanding of the original connotations of the name exemplifies the dangers of an outsider, who is unfamiliar with the indigenous language and tradition, affixing Christian concepts onto foreign words.[16]

Callaway was one of the few to voice disquiet over the widespread use of *Thixo* for the name of God. After making a thorough investigation of the origin of the word, he concluded that it was the praise-name of some 'ancient Hottentot brave'; and declared that it had been 'unwisely and improperly adopted by the early Missionaries; to be explained and excused only on the ground that at first the teachers and the taught were unable freely to communicate ideas to one another'.[17]

Shaw (1860), on the other hand, defended the missionary usage of *Thixo*. He claimed that this appellation was never used by the Xhosa with reference to any other person or being than God, with the exception that, metaphorically, they might say to an individual whom they wished to flatter, ' "You are our *utixo*", meaning their god'.[18] Shaw held that there was but a slight connection between this word and the term used by the Hottentots in their language to denote deity. It was only after long and careful consideration that the missionaries had 'generally concurred in adopting the word *Utixo* as the name for God'. He maintained that throughout the area served by missionaries, from the Colony to beyond the Umzimvubu River, no other meaning was attached to the word by the black people, excepting very rarely in the figurative sense mentioned above; and this was strictly confined to the 'Heathen'. 'No Kaffirs that are under Christian instruction would apply the term even metaphorically in that manner', he said. Shaw ended by criticizing Colenso for trying to 'Kaffrize' a Latin name for God, '*Udio*', which unfortunately in Zulu meant 'a small earthern pot for dishing up food'. Consequently, 'the natives were obliged to explain that the Bishop's *Udio* meant *Utixo*'.[19]

Xhosa Beliefs concerning *Thixo*

The early missionaries found it difficult to get an idea of what the pre-Christian use of the word *Thixo* meant to the Xhosa. Ayliff observed that it was generally used as an invocation or exclamation when someone sneezed, and unless under missionary influence it failed to produce any reverence.[20] An old Xhosa whom Callaway consulted was more explicit. He said that when a man sneezed and used the customary exclamation: 'May *Utikxo* ever regard me with favour,' he associated the praise-name with a supreme power in the above. He elaborated further:

We used to say it when it thundered, and we thus knew
that there is a power which is in heaven; and at length
we adopted the custom of saying, *Utikxo* is he who is
above all. But it was not said that he was in a certain
place in heaven; it was said that he filled the whole
heaven. No distinction of place was made.[21]

Callaway was rightly convinced of Khoi influence on the Xhosa
concept of the supreme being, although it was fervently denied
by his informant. At the same time, there is no suggestion that
the Xhosa adopted the Khoi notion of *Thixo* as the great
ancestor.

Brownlee maintains that the Xhosa undoubtedly held that
the *Thixo* who was preached to them by the missionaries was a
separate and distinct supreme being from *Qamata* and so
accepted the name *Thixo*.[22] In the early 1830s, Kay found that
whereas *Thixo* was generally used among frontier clans for
God, it was seldom used in Mpondoland, showing that the
use of the name was most prevalent in the region where the
Khoi were concentrated and the missionaries first started
work.[23] A hundred years later the spread of missionary influence had resulted in its coming into general use in Mpondoland. Hunter reported that the old people were adamant that
they had always known the word, 'and that they always called
upon *uThixo* when they sneezed, when they were saved from
danger (as in battle), and when laying a stone upon the *izivivane*'.
Further, deformed births were attributed to *uThixo* (*udaliwe
ngho Thixo* – he was created by *uThixo*), and an insane person
was called *umntu kaThixo*, the person of *uThixo*.[24] The Bomvana
are the only group who are reported as being concerned with
the origin of *Thixo*. Their tradition relates that in the beginning
Thixo came out of the sea.[25]

The Satanic Figure: *umTyholi*
Another concept which appears to have been borrowed from
the Khoi is the 'satanic figure' known as *umTyholi*.[26] Kropf
gives the meaning of the word as one who wilfully accuses
another for the purpose of injuring him, a slanderer, the
devil.[27] He is conceived of as an evil spirit found among men,
who can be held responsible for bad and sinful things including

certain bad dispositions shown by men. *umTyholi* is also regarded as the creator of evil things such as poisonous snakes, bats, owls and other objects and creatures connected with witchcraft and sorcery. There is no clear idea about his living place and he is thought to roam the earth. His influence is believed to be confined to the living: he has no power over ancestral spirits.

It is said that the Xhosa had the concept of the evil spirit before the coming of whites; and that it is much stronger among the Rharhabe in Ciskei than among the Gcaleka in Transkei. This lends weight to the supposition that it is of Khoi origin. The more so as the Gqunukhwebe, who are of mixed Gonaqua and Xhosa blood, have the most clearly defined concept of *umTyholi*. As we have seen, the Khoi regarded *//Gaunab* as the source of all evil. All sickness was thought to come from him or his servants, the witches. In Khoi mythology he is in conflict with *Tsui//Goab*, the source of health and prosperity.[28] Satan of Christianity could readily be identified with the concept of *umTyholi*, providing another example of the dynamics in the ongoing process of change in Xhosa religion.

NOTES AND REFERENCES

1. Hahn (1881); Schapera (1965), pp. 376–89. For a general discussion: Callaway (1870), pp. 110–1; Maingard (1934), pp. 135–6; Smith (1950), pp. 92–8. cf. the Tsonga title of *Tilo* which is apparently the personification of the sky: Hammond-Tooke (1974), p. 321.
2. Schapera (1965), pp. 376–8.
3. Hahn (1881), pp. 65, 92, 124; Schapera (1965), p. 378.
4. Hahn gives one form of prayer sung on such occasions: (1881), pp. 58–9.
5. Schapera (1965), pp. 379–81.
6. R. Horton, 'On the Rationality of Conversion', *Africa* 45(3): pp. 226–7, 1975.
7. Entry for 25 September 1799, Van der Kemp's Journal: *Transactions* I, p. 397.
8. Entry for 15 April 1800, ibid., p. 416.
9. Van der Kemp, 'An Account of the Religion . . . of Caffraria', *Transactions* I, p. 432.
10. Ibid.
11. W. H. I. Bleek, 'Researches into the Relations between the Hottentots and Kafirs', *CMM* 1: pp. 200–1. See also Callaway (1870), pp. 105–16.
12. Callaway quoting a Ngqika informant, St Luke's mission station, British Kaffraria, 1875: (1880), p. 94.

13. Entry for 15 April 1800, Van der Kemp's Journal: *Transactions* I, p. 416. Moffat, quoted in *Cape Quarterly Review* I: p. 564 and Callaway (1870), p. 107, also give the meaning as 'one who inflicts pain, or a sore knee'.
14. Brownlee in Thompson (1827), pp. 448–9.
15. *Ti* being the possessive pronoun 'my' and *xwa* meaning 'arm or strength': Ayliff (1846), pp. iv–v.
16. For a discussion on the difficulties involved in finding suitable words in Xhosa to convey Christian concepts: D. Williams, 'The Missionaries on the Eastern Frontier of the Cape Colony 1799–1853' (unpublished Ph.D. thesis, Univ. of Witwatersrand, 1960), pp. 200–1, 292.
17. Callaway (1870), pp. 110, 116.
18. Shaw (1860), p. 451.
19. Ibid., p. 452.
20. Ayliff (1846), p. v. See also Willoughby (1928), p. 181 n. 6.
21. Callaway (1870), pp. 64–5.
22. C. Brownlee, 'A Fragment on Xhosa Religious Beliefs', *African Studies* 14(1): p. 38, 1955.
23. Kay (1833), p. 339.
24. Hunter (1961), p. 270.
25. Cook (n.d.), pp. 103, 106. In 1879, Callaway collected two songs which were supposedly sung by the Xhosa before the coming of the missionaries; and the one refers to 'The Renowned One' coming from beyond the sea in a ship, according to his translation: *S.A. Folk-Lore Journal* II (part 4): pp. 56–60, July 1880.
26. This discussion is based on Malan (1968), pp. 17–19.
27. Kropf and Godfrey (1915), p. 445.
28. Schapera (1965), pp. 387–9.

PART IV

9. CONCLUSION

Changes in the Xhosa Concept of the Supreme Being

We have seen that according to the designations *uMdali*, *uMenzi*, *uHlanga*, *iNkosi yezulu*, *uMvelingqangi* and *uNkulunkulu*, the Xhosa were part of the Nguni tradition in which there were two main conceptions of the supreme being: the one relating to origin and the other connected with the sky and its phenomena. In this monistic world-view we have a background god who is identified as the one who brought man and his animals forth out of the lower world; who reflects both the creative and destructive elements of nature by being both benevolent and malevolent; who is personified as the sky and who manifests his wrath in the natural elements; who is not invoked directly in any way in the day to day life of man, and does not have any moral concern for man; and who is seldom approached. The only occasion on which a ritual was directed to his worship seems to be when man or beast was struck by lightning and a sacrifice was made in propitiation.

Although misfortune was generally interpreted in terms of ancestral punishment or according to witch-beliefs, it is evident that in the closed system of cause and effect typical of the monistic world-view, there were certain areas of the 'inexplicable' which had to be 'explained' in terms of the actions of a remote supernatural power. This is best articulated in the words of Ngqika to Barrow in 1798, when he said 'that they believed in the existence of some invisible power that sometimes brought good and sometimes evil upon them'.[1] The good included the making of 'all those things which they could not understand or imitate', while the evil was related to untimely death and the workings of nature in its 'impersonal, cosmic and more dangerous aspects'.[2]

In addition, we have seen that the designations *Qamata* and *Thixo* were incorporated from the Khoisan, the former possibly centuries ago, the latter towards the end of the 18th century. Ehret notes that a loanword can denote an outright addition to beliefs or else a reconceptualization of an older element.[3] In this instance the former seems to be the case. Loans in the religious sphere may also reflect something about the social history of the people involved. I have shown that the mixing of the Xhosa with the Khoisan opened the way for cultural diffusion, more specifically the infiltration of religious ideas and practices. Intermarriage in particular would have been a powerful influence in fostering the assimilation of new concepts. What is significant for our purposes, however, is the identification of the influences which determined the selection and acceptance of new elements from the incoming tradition by the Xhosa.

It is my contention that the geographical movement and cultural migration of the Xhosa were sufficient to disturb their socio-cultural experience and so create a need to fill an almost unconscious symbol vacuum and to find a new source of power with which to cope with new situations. The more developed Khoisan notions of the supreme being, which involved the active intervention of *Qamata* in human affairs, 'fitted' the Xhosa need and were therefore gradually assimilated into Xhosa belief and practice.

Qamata was invoked in ritual prayer on a variety of different occasions. Mbiti argues that it would be incorrect to assert that the traditional African people generally experienced a spiritual fellowship with God which could approximate the Christian sense of worship. He maintains God was 'utilized' rather than 'worshipped' and the prayers on these occasions were requests to the supreme being 'to give or to do something of a material nature'.[4] These invocations fall within our definition of worship; but in any case the distinction Mbiti makes cannot be maintained in a monistic world-view. On the one hand, all is one and to relate to the immediate is to relate to all if the chain remains unbroken. The sense of this total belonging is an ever present reality, hence the need to maintain the harmony and the role, for example, of the diviner in discovering the locus and cause of any breach. On the other hand, the connections within the monistic world-view are almost mechanistically conceived. For all that nature is experienced as unpredictable, there is always some explanation to be discovered; and a need to assert volition in the supreme being and hence personality essential in the Religion of Secular

World Affirmation, is not to be found yet. In this system, in which everything has its place and purpose, religious ritual to whatever end it may be directed is one of the essential roles of man. *Qamata* was thought of as the ultimate source of power and ritual techniques were either borrowed from the Khoisan, or developed, to approach him in times of national crisis, which were beyond the control of the ancestors. By reason of its nature, this worship of the supreme being was only sporadic and he necessarily stood in a position of 'moral neutrality'. He was a bigger God but he remained within the monistic world-view. The present experience had not yet been sufficiently disturbed as to be unacceptable and so precipitate a move towards transcendence.

The praise-names *Qamata* and *Thixo* appear to have had similar connotations originally so that it was not surprising that *Thixo* gradually superseded *Qamata* following the increasing interaction between Xhosa and Khoi. With the adoption of *Thixo* by the missionaries for the Christian concept of God, the name became identified with the move from monism to monotheism and an increasing sense of the transcendence of God, although it is clear that two sets of meaning must have existed side by side for a considerable length of time. Other instances of missionary influence have been indicated at the relevant points throughout the text.

The Move to the Concept of a Transcendent Deity

In what Cumpsty calls the Religion of Secular World Affirmation, the divine is no longer identified with present experience, pervading it and maintaining it, but will be above it and beyond it. There is both a spatial and a temporal dimension in the symbol of transcendence. God is understood as being wholly other and higher than we are. He is also to be known in the future, not the past, for he is the God out in front leading us on. Transcendence brings with it a concept of the world as having a beginning and an end and therefore a linear dimension of time. For there to be a radical gap between God and man the beginning must be *creatio ex nihilo*. As an act of divine will creation must also have a purpose or destiny. The discovery of a future dimension of time brings with it a sense of history moving towards an ultimate fulfilment. Time is therefore no longer cyclical but linear, running from creation to destiny. Because the world has a beginning and does not share in the divine eternity, it is therefore secular; and only in a secularized world can man think of himself as free to shape the environment.

In this directional world-view the character of God is seen to be more significant than his power. God's character becomes known through revelation and while revelation does take place in creation it is chiefly through history. This has to be a monotheistic religion because if there is more than one divinity there would be confusion and, as with dualism, it would not be possible to interpret God's initiation and control of historic events. Nevertheless, God's character can be perceived in different ways. In Christianity there is an emphasis on divine love and this brings with it freedom and responsibility. A transcendent deity must be personal. He is beyond manipulation of man and cannot be conceived as impersonal. The form of religion therefore is covenant and co-operation with the divine in a historical destiny. Cumpsty describes the ideal man in this type of religion as being:

> no longer one who passively fits himself into the rhythms of nature or withdraws from it but one who actively takes hold of his real, secular and essentially good environment and seeks to shape it in conformity to what he understands to be the divine will. This is necessarily a corporate symbol, the kingdom as its goal.[5]

The Present Use of the God-name *Qamata*

Most Xhosa Christians affirm a universal concept of the Creator.[6] In addition, many argue that the *Qamata* whom they have always known is the same as the Christian God. There is a strong move today to replace the name *Thixo*, which is regarded as having been foisted on them by the missionaries, with *Qamata*. This conforms with the desire to recover past traditions and customs as part of the black cultural renaissance, and goes together with the resurgence of the ancestor cult.[7]

The Ciskei government has taken a strong lead in trying to foster cultural pride; but although the term *Qamata* is sometimes mentioned in the religious context, the references leave the conceptualization of this God-name undefined and it is not certain whether it is the name or the concept that is most important in the idea of developing an 'African form of religion', nor what the concept would include. So for example, the Minister of Education in 1979, Chief D. M. Jongilanga, is quoted as telling a large group of teachers at Zwelitsha that the type of religion given to blacks by the missionaries was alien to them. 'There is a need for our own form of religion based on our culture and tradition', the chief said.[8] That same year Chief L. W. Maqoma, the Ciskei Minister of the Interior, made a speech in which he appealed for Christian unity, 'in the African sense of worshipping their God, *Qamata*'.[9] The vagueness of these references points to the fact that once again *Qamata* is a carrier of change.

The name *Qamata* is also linked with the peasant revolts in Transkei in the late 1950s and early 1960s which gave rise to the so-called *Poqo* campaign in the Rand, the Cape Peninsula and Queenstown. In November 1967, a trial took place relating to an attempt on the life of Chief K. D. Matanzima at Cofimvaba by a group of men from Paarl and Langa. A State witness testified that in 1961 he had joined *Poqo* and its 'sort-of-church *Qamata*'.[10] In contrast, Mafeje, who monitored the political rallies in Langa in 1960, observed that 'for the younger generation, especially in the urban areas, the African God is a complete mystery, and the Christian God an anomaly'. He went on to say that one of the speakers made an impassioned speech, 'appealing to the "African national God", which turned out to be "the god of Moshoeshoe, the god of Hintsa the god of Tshaka and the god of Tshekedi", in other words, the gods of the four most respected South African tribal chiefs'. Mafeje questioned whether this was hero-worshipping or ancestor cult.[11]

Again these references are merely an indication of how the God-name *Qamata* is used by some Xhosa today; and of how conceptions of the supreme being can vary depending in what tradition a person stands. Moreover, there is an overlapping between the traditionalist conception, the Christian conception and an 'African consciousness'.

It seems to me that although there can be continuity with tradition in the African expression of Christianity, and indeed the religious quest is always the same, there is a failure to perceive that a move towards symbolizing the experience of that ultimate reality as transcendent implies a radical break with the background god of the monistic world-view. For although the quest remains the same, the social and personal consequences of the change in symbols are dramatic, as for example the protagonists of Weber's Calvinism-Capitalism hypothesis have been at pains to point out. It is not a case of all have run and all must have a prize; but the debate having taken place on two levels: that of experience and that of the symbolization of experience. And in the sense that the experience is primary, the African opinion is right in asserting pre-Christian experience of the supreme being, but the immense consequences of a shift in symbols is ignored at our peril.

Not least among the perils is the established Churches' attitude to transitional religious movements. If one is going to stand firmly for the traditional Christian symbols, one needs to recognise that the experience to which they refer may well make these symbols, as Mafeje says, anomalous. The different world-views of a people caught in transition between two cultures may appear to be wide apart, but I suggest that if one looks at the symbol system popularly in use it can be seen that there is after all not such a wide gap between the world-views they represent.

A study of the faith-healing movement of Mrs Flora Ludlolo, known as Ma-Radebe, at Cancele in Transkei is a case in point, for the evidence indicates that no clearcut divisions can be drawn between different religious affiliations among black people.[12] No matter whether they claim allegiance to the symbol systems of traditionalist, main-line Christian or Zionist, their world-views are permeated by the thought-patterns and symbolism of the pre-Christian period. In other words, there continues to be a sense of cosmic oneness which draws little or no distinction between sacred and secular, natural and super-

106

natural: the belief system continues to be explanatory, with misfortune being interpreted within a closed system of cause and effect; and well-being still consists in keeping in harmony with the cosmic totality.

Ma-Radebe incorporates Christian elements in her healing services, and the intention is to give the words and action a Christian orientation, but the meaning of the symbols, Christian and traditional alike, draw their power from the African tradition and are merely reinforced by the Christian tradition. The ritual carries with it the authority of the magico-religious tradition of the African past, and this authority is carried over to the new symbols. The symbols she uses are therefore a meeting point because they can be variously interpreted according to different religious affiliations and so fit a wide experience. The Catholicism of medieval or peasant Christianity, with its much maligned syncretism with 'superstitious practices', surely represents a comparable intermediate stage in those cultures. That Ma-Radebe is able to answer the needs of a people who find themselves in a mixed culture, being willing to meet them where they are, provides a challenge to the Churches.

Without wishing to diminish the personal and social significance of symbols, or of the stability and continuity provided only by an institution committed to a particular symbol set, it is nevertheless the case that the God a people worship is the God who is real in their own experience and indeed must always be so if he is to be the Living God.

NOTES AND REFERENCES

1. See note 127: Barrow II (1804), p. 214.
2. For a discussion on comparative beliefs among the Bantu-speaking peoples of Southern Africa see Hammond-Tooke (1974), pp. 320–1.
3. Ehret in Ranger and Kimambo (1972), p. 46.
4. J. S. Mbiti, *New Testament Eschatology in an African Background. A Study of the Encounter between New Testament Theology and African Traditional Concepts* (London, 1971), pp. 94–5.
5. This discussion is based on Cumpsty's 'Model of Religious Change', *Religion in Southern Africa* 1(2): pp. 60–61, July 1980, and 'Report on the C.P.S.A. Commission' (U.C.T., 1981).
6. E.g. Interview with B. Somhlahlo, Fort Hare, 25 October 1978.

7. C. W. Manona, 'The Resurgence of the Ancestor Cult among Xhosa Christians' (unpublished paper, Lumko, January 1981).
8. *Indaba*, supplement to *Daily Dispatch*, 2 November 1979.
9. *Indaba*, 5 January 1979. The African conception of God, even into and through Christianity, has been widely reported in other parts of Africa. See for example N. Mushete, 'Authenticity and Christianity in Zaire', p. 233, and S. G. Kibicho, 'The continuity of the African conception of God into and through Christianity: a Kikuyu case-study', pp. 370–88, in *Christianity in Independent Africa*, edited by E. Fasholé-Luke *et al.* (London, 1978).
10. *Cape Times*, 9 November 1967. I am indebted to T. Lodge of the Department of Political Science, University of the Witwatersrand for this information.
11. A. Mafeje, 'Religion, Class and Ideology in South Africa' in *Religion and Social Change in Southern Africa*, edited by M. G. Whisson and M. West (London and Cape Town, 1975), p. 176.
12. J. Hodgson, 'The Faith-Healer of Cancele: some problems in analysing religious experience among black people' (Paper presented to the Fourth Conference of the Association for the History of Religion (Southern Africa), University of Natal, Pietermaritzburg, June 1982).

APPENDIX I

The Distribution of Animals, etc., etc., after the Creation, as related by a Kafir

Contributed by Thomas Bain to the South African Folk-Lore Journal II (Part 2): pp. 21–3, March 1880.

Teco (*uThixo*) had every description of stock and property. There were three nations created, viz., the whites, the *Amakosa* or Kafirs, and the *Amalouw* or Hottentots. A day was appointed for them to appear before the *Teco* to receive whatever he might apportion to each tribe. While they were assembling, a honey bird, or honey guide, came fluttering by, and all the Hottentots ran after it, whistling and making the peculiar noise they generally do while following this wonderful little bird. The *Teco* remonstrated with them about their behaviour, but to no purpose. He thereupon denounced them as a vagrant race that would have to exist on wild roots and honey beer, and possess no stock whatever.

When the fine herds of cattle were brought, the Kafirs became very much excited – the one exclaiming, 'That black and white cow is mine!' and another, 'That red cow and black bull are mine!' and so on, till at last the *Teco*, whose patience had been severely taxed by their shouts and unruly behaviour, denounced them as a restless people, who would only possess cattle.

The whites patiently waited until they received cattle, horses, sheep, and all sorts of property. Hence, the old Kafir observed, 'You whites have got every thing. We Kafirs have only cattle, while the *Amalouw* or Hottentots have nothing.'*

---

* Bain adds a note to the effect that the story had been related to him many years previously.

APPENDIX II

Of the Creation of People

An undated manuscript (mid 19th century?) by William Kekale Kaye, 'a native interpreter': MS 172c, Grey Collection, South African Library.

There were four persons in the beginning. They were God and Satan. God was the Chief and Satan was cook. There were four houses, one was that of the Chief, one was a cook house, one in which the Chief worked, the other was a round house made of grass in which two persons lived.

A man was first created. He was made of earth and a cloud mixed together by means of which man became a substance which did not wither as trees do. When he had completed man he made him to fall asleep on his right side, and took out the short rib, with which he mixed cloud and moon and made woman, which is the cause of women having monthly illness regularly happening each month.

It one day happened that the man went out into the fields to look at the cattle, which were not then folded as they were the only animals then existing (or rather they were the only animals from which they obtained food). On returning home he went to the left side of the house with a log of wood on his shoulder, when he found that Satan had been in the house with the woman, and had endeavoured to win her to his purposes. But she rejected his advances saying the Chief said I was only to live with the man whom I have, but I had no instruction concerning this. Satan said I would have shown you the tree of which the Chief God eats, by which he is so wise.

The woman said pray tell me, do show it me, but Satan said no, let us first lie together. The woman refused, and Satan went away to seek it, and returned with it, and said what do you say now. I have it do you consent. On this the woman consented and they lay together. But he only made her long for the fruit without permitting her to taste it, till at last he put some in her mouth as if it were particles of ants and said, the

110

man who walks with the Chief says this is tree of which he eats. And it was nice. She put by some for her husband. When the husband came he looked in at the door and said why does the woman to-day for the first time cover herself. He said why is it they were naked and were not ashamed. The woman said you are a man who talks too fast, cannot you sit down and listen to me. He sat down, and she told him how that Satan had been there and showed her the tree of which the Chief ate. She took out the piece she had saved for him, saying here it is, taste how delicious it is. The man refused, saying this is the tree of which the Chief said we were not to eat of. What is this you have done? She urged him saying do but taste one mouthful. At length he took one and swallowed it, it stuck fast in his 'Adam's apple' where it remained. This is the cause of men's having 'Adam's apple' and of their loud tone of voice.

After this the chief came and looked into the door. They were alarmed and hid themselves. He left and returned next day, and called them out to the front and said what is this you have done. They denied saying no we have done nothing. The Chief said although I ask you I am not one who requires to be told by any one for I see all things of myself. They said yes Chief we have eaten the tree of which you said we were not to eat. We were tempted by Satan.

He said to them to-day having eaten it you will suffer pain, you shall work in order to obtain food, you woman you shall suffer in pregnancy, and death following. You shall find yourself with child and miscarry. When you have borne a child he shall die. From to-day they shall be subject to suffering and death. This is fixed and it is your lot.

APPENDIX III

List of God-names

Translation of names by Professor H. W. Pahl, Mr O. B. Mpondo and Mr T. A. Ndungane of the Xhosa Dictionary Project, University of Fort Hare; and Father A. Fischer of McKay's Nek Mission, Transkei.

iNkosi yeenkosi	The Chief of Chiefs: Lord of Lords
iNkosi enkulu	The Great Chief
iNkosi yezulu	The Chief or Lord of the Sky
Mdalidiphu	Creator of the Deep (coined by Nxele/Makhanda)
Ophezu konke	The One who is above all others: The Highest
Osenyangweni	The One who is in the highest or in heaven: The Highest
Osenyangwaneni	Older form of the Highest
ubuThathu obuNgcwele	The Holy Trinity
uDali	The Creator, Moulder, Maker (this form is only used in Xhosa to refer to the supreme being)
uDuma-barhwaqele	Great noise – when it roars/ thunders the people cringe or shrink with fear (a praise-name of the Xhosa Paramount Hintsa)
uGquma-barhwaqele	When he roars the people shrink with fear
uHlanga	The Source or Origin of Life (associated with the cosmogonic myth)
uHlathi lenyaniso	The Forest of Truth: The Refuge of Truth (a praise-name for God used by Ntsikana in his Great Hymn, *Ulo Thixo Omkhulu*)

112

uKhaka lenyaniso	The Shield of Truth (a praise-name for God used by Ntsikana in his Great Hymn)
uKumkani wookumkani	The King of Kings
uMbangi yobom	The Cause of Life (One who caused): The Originator of Life
uMdali	The Creator, Moulder, Maker (also in general use)
uMenzi	The Maker of all things: The One who brings things about: The Creator
uMenzi weenkwenkwezi	The Creator of the Stars (in Ntsikana's Great Hymn)
uMgwebi	The Judge, at the day of judgement (resurrection)
uMhlanganisi wemihlambi eyalanayo	The One who brings together all the different herds who are rejecting one another (in Ntsikana's Great Hymn)
uMlawuli weento zonke	The Ruler of all things
uMniki weento zonke	The Giver of all things
uMnini-nto-zonke	The Owner of all things
uMthombo wobomi	The Source of Life
uMtriniti	The Trinity
uNdikhoyo	The-I-am-the-One-who-always-exists/is-ever-present (Moses and the Burning Bush)
uNdinguye	The-I-am-the-One (Moses and the Burning Bush)
Ndinguye eNdinguye	I am who I am (as above)
uNdlovenomxhaka	The Elephant with the ivory armlet: the Great One (praise-name of Hintsa; the ivory armlet is worn above the elbow by a chief or one on whom this honour is conferred by a chief. Elephants are also associated with chiefs.)

113

uNgcwele-kathathu	The Threefold Holy One
uNgcwele-ntathu	The Threefold Holy One
uNqin' ezingel' -imiphefumlo	The Hunting Expedition which hunts souls: The Hunter of Souls (in Ntsikana's Great Hymn)
uNgubenkulu	The Big Blanket; He covers everybody to protect them: The Great Protector (in Ntsikana's Great Hymn, said to be taken from the Khoi word *Gqub/ !Gub* meaning cloud-cover: Hahn (1881), p. 64)
uNkulunkulu	The Greatest (thought to be of Zulu origin and applied only to the supreme being)
uNqaba yenyaniso	The Fortress of Truth (in Ntsikana's Great Hymn)
uQamata	God-name of Khoisan origin
uSifuba-sibanzi	Broad-Breast (said to have been coined by Ntsikana as the name for Christ)
uSimakade	The One who remains or stands for ever The Eternal One
uSobom	Father of Life
uSobubomi	Father of Life (different grammatical form)
uSobubele	Father of Kindness
uSokukhanya	Father/Source of Light
uSolufefe	Father of Grace
uSoluthando	Father of Love
uSolwazi	Father of Knowledge (The Omniscient)
uSomandla	Powerful Father: The Almighty
uSombawo	The Great Father
uSomkhulu	The Great Father: The Great One
uSonini-nanini	Father for Ever and Ever: The Eternal

uSosisa	Father of Generosity
uSozinceba	The Merciful Father
uTayi	Name for the Son of God (coined by Nxele)
uTayi omkhulu wezihlwele	The Great Tayi of the multitude
uThixo	God-name of Khoi (origin derived from Tsui//Goab)
uYehova	Jehovah
uZiqu-zithathu	The One of Three bodies: The Three Persons of God

BIBLIOGRAPHY

I Unpublished manuscripts

Burton, A. W.: 'The Cattle-Killing Movement 1856–57' (lecture at Grahams-town, 1946, Cory Library, Rhodes University).

Kaye, W. K.: 'Of the Creation of People' and 'Xhosa History', MS 172c, n.d. (Grey Collection, South African Library).

Mpotokwane, J.: 'Native Folklore,' MS 1228, n.d. (Cory Library, Rhodes University).

II Unpublished theses and papers

Bettison, D. G.: 'The Cosmology of the Southern Bantu' (Dissertation, Rhodes University, 1954).

Bigalke, E. H.: 'The Religious System of the Ndlambe of East London District' (M.A., Rhodes University, 1969).

Cumpsty, J. S.: 'Report on the C.P.S.A. Commission to Investigate the Pastoral, Practical, Theological Challenge posed by Marxism in Africa' (MS, U.C.T., 1981).

Dwane, S.: 'Christianity in Relation to Xhosa Religion' (Ph.D., University of London, 1979).

Falati, N.: 'The Story of Ntsikana: a Gaika Xhosa' (translated by C. Falati and C. Mpaki, St Mark's, 1895. MS, Cory Library, Rhodes University).

Hodgson, J.: 'The Faith-Healer of Cancele: some Problems in Analysing Religious Experience among Black People' (paper presented to the Fouth Conference of A.H.R.S.A., University of Natal, Pietermaritzburg, June 1982).

Kagame, A.: 'La philosophie bantu rwandaise de l'être' (Ph.D., Rome, 1956).

Kuckertz, H.: 'A Symbol that Interprets the World: Ancestor Cult and Ceremonially Drinking Beer in Mthwa Society' (paper, Lumko, 1981).

Malan, J. S.: 'Die Tradisionele Religie van die Xhosa' (M.A., Unisa, 1968).

Manona, C. W.: 'The Resurgence of the Ancestor Cult among Xhosa Christians' (paper, Lumko, 1981).

Moorcroft, E.: 'Theories of Millenarianism Considered with Reference to certain South African Movements' (B. Letters, Oxford, 1967).

Nkonki, G.: 'The Traditional Prose Literature of the Ngqika' (M.A., Unisa, 1968).

Pahl, H. W.: 'List of Xhosa God-names,' Personal Communication, 18 October 1978.

Peires, J. B.: 'A History of the Xhosa c 1700–1835' (M.A., Rhodes University, 1976. Published in part in *The House of Phalo*, Johannesburg, 1981).

Vilakazi, B. W.: 'The Oral and Written Literature in Nguni' (D.Litt., University of the Witwatersrand, 1946).

Williams, D.: 'The Missionaries on the Eastern Frontier of the Cape Colony 1799–1853' (Ph.D., University of the Witwatersrand, 1960).

III General literature

Alberti, L.: *Ludwig Alberti's Account of the Tribal Life and Customs of the Xhosa in 1807* (1810; trans. W. Fehr, Cape Town, 1968).

Appleyard, J. W.: *The Kafir Language* (King William's Town, 1850).

Argyle, J. and Preston-Whyte, E. (eds.): *Social System and Tradition in South Africa: Essays in Honour of Eileen Krige* (Cape Town, 1978).

Ashton, E. H.: *The Basuto* (London, 1952).

Ayliff, J.: *A Vocabulary of the Kafir Language* (London, 1846).

Backhouse, J.: *Narrative of a Visit to the Mauritius and South Africa* (London, 1844).

Barrow, J.: *An Account of Travels into the Interior of Southern Africa, 1797 and 1798, 1804* (2 vols., London 1801 and 1804).

Baumann, H.: *Schöpfung und Urzeit des Menschen im Mythus der Afrikanischen Völker* (Berlin, 1936).

Beier, U.: *The Origin of Life and Death* (London, 1966).

Berglund, A.-I.: *Zulu Thought-Patterns and Symbolism* (London, 1976).

Bleek, W. H. I.: *Zulu Legends* (Pretoria, 1952).

Bokwe, J. K.: *Ntsikana: the Story of an African Convert* with an Appendix, *Ibali Lika Ntsikana* (2nd ed., Lovedale, 1914).

Bourke, M.: *Badoli the Ox* (Cape Town, n.d.).

Brownlee, C.: *Reminiscences of Kaffir Life and History* (Lovedale, 1896).

Brownlee, F.: *The Transkeian Native Territories: Historical Records* (Lovedale, 1923).

Bryant, A. T.: *A Zulu-English Dictionary* (Marianhill, 1905).

———*The Zulu People* (Pietermaritzburg, 1949).

Bud-M'Belle, I.: *Kafir Scholar's Companion* (London, 1903).

Callaway, H.: *Nursery Tales, Traditions, and Histories of the Zulus* (London, 1868).

———*The Religious System of the Amazulu* (London, 1870).

Campbell, J.: *Travels in South Africa, 1813* (London, 1815).

———*Travels in South Africa . . . being a Narrative of a Second Journey, 1820* (2 vols., London, 1822).

Casalis, E.: *The Basutos* (London, 1861).

Chanaiwa, D. (ed.): *Profiles in Self-Determination. African Responses to European Colonialism in Southern Africa 1652 – Present* (Northridge, 1976).

Chalmers, J. A.: *Tiyo Soga. A Page of South African Mission Work* (Edinburgh and London, 1877).

Colenso, J. W.: *Ten Weeks in Natal* (Cambridge, 1855).

———*Zulu-English Dictionary* (Pietermaritzburg, 1861 and 1884).

Cook, P. A. W.: *The Social Organization and Ceremonial Institutions of the Bomvana* (Cape Town, n.d.).

Damberger, C. F.: *Travels in the Interior of Africa from the Cape of Good Hope to Morocco, from the years 1781 to 1797* (London, 1801).

Daneel, M. L.: *The God of the Matopo Hills* (The Hague, 1970).

Davis, W. J.: *Dictionary of the Kafir Language* (London, 1872).

Derricourt, R. M.: *Prehistoric Man in the Ciskei and Transkei* (Cape Town and Johannesburg, 1977).

Döhne, J. L.: *Das Kaffernland und Seine Bewohner* (Berlin, 1844).

———*A Zulu-Kafir Dictionary* (Cape Town, 1857).

Doke, C. M. and Vilakazi, B. W.: *Zulu-English Dictionary* (Johannesburg, 1948).

Douglas, M.: *Purity and Danger: an analysis of concepts of pollution and taboos* (London, 1966).

———*Natural Symbols* (London, 1970).

Elphick, R.: *Kraal and Castle: Khoikhoi and the Founding of White South Africa* (New Haven and London, 1977).

Evans-Pritchard, E. E.: *Nuer Religion* (London, 1956).

Fasholé-Luke, E., Gray, R., Hastings, A. and Tasie, G. (eds.): *Christianity in Independent Africa* (London, 1978).

Fawcett, T.: *The Symbolic Language of Religion* (London, 1970).

Finnegan, R.: *Oral Literature in Africa* (Oxford, 1970).

Gardiner, A.: *Narrative of a Journey to the Zoolu Country in South Africa* (London, 1836).

Godfrey, R.: *Bird-lore of the Eastern Cape Province* (Johannesburg, 1941).

Hahn, T.: *Tsuni-//Goam, the Supreme Being of the Khoi-Khoi* (London, 1881).

Hammond-Tooke, W. D.: *Bhaca Society* (Cape Town, 1962).

———(ed.): *The Bantu-Speaking Peoples of Southern Africa* (2nd ed., London, 1974).

Hewat, M. L.: *Bantu Folk Lore* (Cape Town, n.d.).

Hodgson, J.: *Ntsikana's 'Great Hymn': a Xhosa Expression of Christianity in the Early 19th Century Eastern Cape* (Centre for African Studies, U.C.T., Communication no. 4, 1980).

Holden, W. C.: *The Past, Present and Future of the Kaffir Races* (London, 1866).

Holt, B.: *Joseph Williams and the Pioneer Mission to the South-Eastern Bantu* (Lovedale, 1954).

Hunter, M.: *Reaction to Conquest: Effects of Contact with Europeans on the Pondo of South Africa* (London, 1st ed. 1936, 2nd ed. 1961).

Idowu, E. B.: *African Traditional Religion: a Definition* (London, 1973).

———*Olódùmarè: God in Yoruba Belief* (London, 1962).

Inskeep, R. R.: *The Peopling of Southern Africa* (Cape Town and London, 1978).

Jahn, J.: *Muntu: an Outline of the New African Culture* (New York, 1961).

Jenkinson, T. B.: *Amazulu: the Zulus, their Past History, Manners, Customs and Language* (London, 1882).

Junod, H. A.: *The Life of a South African Tribe* (2 vols., rev. ed. London, 1927).

Junod, H. P.: *Bantu Heritage* (Johannesburg, 1938).

Kay, S.: *Travels and Researchers in Caffraria* (London, 1833).

Kidd, D.: *The Essential Kafir* (London, 1904).

Kolb, P.: *The Present State of the Cape of Good Hope* (London, 1731).

Krige, E. J.: *The Social System of the Zulus* (London, 1936).

———and Krige, J. D.: *The Realm of a Rain-Queen* (London, 1943).

Kropf, A.: *Das Volk der Xosa-Kaffern im östlichen Südafrika* (Berlin, 1889).

———and Godfrey, R.: *A Kafir-English Dictionary* (2nd ed. edited by R. Godfrey, 1915).

Laubscher, B. J. F.: *Sex, Custom and Psychopathology* (London, 1937).

Leslie, D.: *Among the Zulus and Amatongas* (London, 1875).

Le Vaillant, F.: *Travels into the Interior Parts of Africa by way of the Cape of Good Hope in the years 1780, 81, 82, 83, 84 and 85* (2 vols., London, 1790).

Lichtenstein, H.: *Travels in Southern Africa in the Years 1803, 1804, 1805* (2 vols., 1812–15; reprinted V.R.S. 10, Cape Town, 1928–30).

Lienhardt, D.: *Divinity and Experience. The Religion of the Dinka* (Oxford, 1961).

Livingstone, D.: *Missionary Travels and Researches in South Africa* (London, 1857).

Louw, J. A.: *The Nomenclature of Cattle in the South-Eastern Bantu Languages* (Communications of Unisa, C2, 1957).

Maclean, J. (Compiler): *A Compendium of Kafir Laws and Customs* (Cape Town, 1866).

Mbiti, J. S.: *African Religions and Philosophy* (London, 1969).

———*Concepts of God in Africa* (London, 1970).

———*New Testament Eschatology in an African Background: a Study of the Encounter between New Testament Theology and African Traditional Concepts* (London, 1971).

———*The Prayers of African Religion* (London, 1975).

McKay, J.: *The Origin of the Xosa and others* (Cape Town, 1911).

McLaren, J.: *A Xhosa Grammar* (London, 1940).

McVeigh, M. J.: *God in Africa: Conceptions of God in African Traditional Religion and Christianity* (Massachusetts, 1974).

Moffat, R.: *Missionary Labours and Scenes in Southern Africa* (London, 1842).

Moodie, D.: *The Record: or a series of Official Papers relative to the Condition and Treatment of the Native Tribes of South Africa* (1840; reprint ed., Amsterdam and Cape Town, 1960).

Mossop, E. (ed.): *The Journal of Hendrik Jacob Wikar (1779) . . . and of Jacobus Coetsé Jansz (1760) and Willem van Reenen (1791)* (Cape Town, 1935).

Mqhayi, S. K.: *U-Mqhayi wase-Ntab'ozuko* (Lovedale, 1939).

Ndawo, H. M.: *Uhambo luka Gqoboka* (Lovedale, n.d.).

Ngubane, H.: *Body and Mind in Zulu Medicine* (London, 1977).

Nienaber, G. S. and Raper, P.: *Toponymica Hottentotica* (Pretoria, 1977 and 1980).

Oliver, R. (ed.): *Cambridge History of Africa* (Cambridge, 1977).

Pauw, B. A.: *Religion in a Tswana Chiefdom* (London, 1960).

———*Christianity and Xhosa Tradition. Beliefs and Ritual among Xhosa-speaking Christians* (Cape Town, 1975).

Peires, J. B.: *The House of Phalo* (Johannesburg, 1981).

Pringle, T.: *Narrative of a Residence in South Africa* (London, 1835).

Ranger, T. O. and Kimambo, I. N. (eds.): *The Historical Study of African Religion* (Berkeley and Los Angeles, 1972).

Raum, O. F. and de Jager, E. J.: *Transition and Change in a Rural Community* (Fort Hare, 1972).

Ray, B. C.: *African Religions: Symbol, Ritual and Community* (New Jersey, 1976).

Rose, C.: *Four Years in Southern Africa* (London, 1829).

Rubusana, W. B.: *Zemk'iinkomo Magwalandini* (abridged ed., Lovedale, 1966).

Saunders, C. and Derricourt, R. (eds.): *Beyond the Cape Frontier: Studies in the History of the Transkei and Ciskei* (London, 1974).

Sawyerr, H.: *God: Ancestor or Creator? Aspects of the Traditional belief in Ghana, Nigeria and Sierra Leone* (London, 1970).

Samuelson, L. H.: *Some Zulu Customs and Folk-Lore* (London, 1912).

Schapera, I. (ed.): *The Bantu-Speaking Tribes of South Africa* (Cape Town, 1937).

———(ed.): *The Early Cape Hottentots* (Cape Town, 1933).

———*The Khoisan Peoples of South Africa: Bushmen and Hottentots* (London, 1965).

Setiloane, G. M.: *The Image of God among the Sotho-Tswana* (Rotterdam, 1976).

Shaw, W.: *The Story of my Mission in South-Eastern Africa* (London, 1860).

Shooter, J.: *The Kafirs of Natal and the Zulu Country* (London, 1857).

Shorter, A.: *African Christian Theology: Adaptation or Incarnation* (London, 1975).

Soga, J. H.: *The South-Eastern Bantu* (Johannesburg, 1930).

———*The Ama-Xosa: Life and Customs* (Lovedale, n.d., 1931?).

Soga, T. B.: *Intlalo ka Xhosa* (Lovedale, 1936).

Smith, E. W. (ed.): *African Ideas of God* (London, 1950).

Sparrman, A.: *A Voyage to the Cape of Good Hope, 1772–6* (2 vols., Dublin, 1785).

Stayt, H.: *The Bavenda* (London, 1931).

Steedman, A.: *Wanderings and Adventures in the Interior of Southern Africa* (London, 1835).

Stow, G. W.: *The Native Races of South Africa* (London, 1905).

Taylor, J. V.: *The Primal Vision: Christian Presence amid African Religion* (London, 1963).

Tempels, P.: *Bantu Philosophy* (Paris, 1969).

Theal, G. M.: *Kaffir Folk Lore* (London, 1882).

———*Ethnography and Condition of South Africa before 1505* (London, 1910).

Thompson, G.: *Travels and Adventures in Southern Africa* (2 vols., London, 1827).

Thompson, L. (ed.): *African Societies in Southern Africa* (London, 1969).

Thunberg, C. R.: *Travels in Europe, Africa and Asia made between the years 1770 and 1779* (2 vols., 2nd ed. London, 1795).

Tyler, J.: *Forty Years Among the Zulus* (Boston and Chicago, 1891; facsimile reprint, Cape Town, 1971).

Wallis, S. J. (ed.): *Inkolo Namasiko aBantu* (London, 1930).

Wauchope, I.: *The Natives and their Missionaries* (Lovedale, 1908).

Werner, A.: *Myths and Legends of the Bantu* (London, 1933).

Williams, D.: *Umfundisi: a Biography of Tiyo Soga 1829–1871* (Lovedale, 1978).

Willoughby, W. C.: *The Soul of the Bantu* (London, 1928).

———*Nature-Worship and Taboo* (Hartford, 1932).

Wilson, M.: *Religion and the Transformation of Society: a Study in Social Change in Africa* (Cambridge, 1971).

Wilson, M. and Thompson, L. (eds.): *The Oxford History of South Africa* (2 vols., Oxford, 1969).

IV Articles

'A Native Lad': 'A Native Legend of the Origin of Men and Animals,' *The Christian Express* XXXIII(395), pp. 122–3, 1 August, 1903.

A Student at Zonnebloem College: 'Some Native Beliefs,' *Zonnebloem College Magazine* 3(12), p. 9, Easter 1905.

Anon: 'Notes on Star Lore,' *The Cape Quarterly Review* I, pp. 53–5, October, 1881.

Bain, T.: 'The Distribution of Animals, etc., etc., after the Creation, as related by a Kafir,' *South African Folk-Lore Journal* II (part 2), pp. 21–3, March, 1880.

Beiderbecke, H.: 'Some Religious Ideas and Customs of the Ovaherero,' *South African Folk-Lore Journal* II (part 5), pp. 93–7, September, 1880.

Bengston, D. R.: 'Three African Religious Founders,' *Journal of Religion in Africa* VII (fasc. 1), pp. 16–26, 1975.

Bennie, J.: Letter dated 20 March 1822, *Report of the Glasgow Missionary Society*, Appendix, p. 29, 1822.

Birmingham, D. and Marks, S.: 'Southern Africa,' in *Cambridge History of Africa* III, edited by R. Oliver (Cambridge, 1977).

Bleek, W. H. I.: 'Researches into the Relations between the Hottentots and Kafirs,' *Cape Monthly Magazine* 1, pp. 200–1, 1880.

Bokwe, J. K.: 'Remarks,' *G.66–'83, Report on Proceedings with Appendices on the Government Commission on Native Laws and Customs*, 1883, Appendix B, pp. 20–1.

Bourquin, W.: 'Click Words which Xhosa, Zulu and Sotho have in common,' *African Studies* (10–11), pp. 59–81, 1951–2.

Brownlee, C.: 'A fragment on Xhosa Religious Beliefs,' *African Studies* XIV(1), pp. 37–41, 1955.

————'Notes' in *A Compendium of Kafir Laws and Customs* (Cape Town, 1866).

Brownlee, F.: 'Burial Places of Chiefs,' *African Affairs* 43, p. 23, 1944.

Brownlee, J.: 'Account of the Amakosae, or Southern Caffres,' Appendix to *Travels and Adventures in Southern Africa* II, by G. Thompson (London, 1827).

Callaway, H.: 'South African Folk-Lore,' *Cape Monthly Magazine* n.s. 16, pp. 109–10, 1878.

————'On the Religious Sentiment amongst the Tribes of South Africa,' *Cape Monthly Magazine* 2, pp. 92–3, 1880.

Cumpsty, J. S.: 'A Model of Religious Change in Socio-Cultural Disturbance,' *Religion in Southern Africa* 1(2), pp. 59–70, July 1980.

'D': 'Reminiscences of an old Kafir,' *Cape Monthly Magazine* 3, pp. 289–94, 1880.

Dammann, E.: 'Die Religiöse Bedeutung das Bantuworstammes – Lungu,' *Ex Orbe Religionum* (1922).

————'A Tentative Philological Typology of some African High Deities,' *Journal of Religion in Africa* II, pp. 81–95, 1969.

Dapper, O.: 'Kaffraria or the Land of the Kafirs also named Hottentots (1668),' in *The Early Cape Hottentots*, edited by I. Schapera (Cape Town, 1933).

Dart, R.: 'Rock Engravings,' *South African Journal of Science* XXVIII, pp. 475–86, 1931.

Derricourt, R. M.: 'Settlement in the Transkei and Ciskei before the Mfecane,' in *Beyond the Cape Frontier*, edited by C. Saunders and R. Derricourt (London, 1974).

Edwards: 'Tradition of the Bayeye,' *South African Folk-Lore Journal* II (part 2), pp. 34–7, March 1880.

Ehret, C.: 'Language evidence and Religious History' in *The Historical Study of African Religion*, edited by T. O. Ranger and I. N. Kimambo (Berkeley and Los Angeles, 1972).

Gqoba, W.: 'The Native Tribes, their Laws, Customs and Beliefs,' *The Christian Express* XV(179), p. 93, 1 June 1885.

Grevenbroek, J. G.: 'An Elegant and Accurate Account of the African Race living round the Cape of Good Hope commonly called Hottentots (1695)' in *The Early Cape Hottentots*, edited by I. Schapera (Cape Town, 1933).

Hahn, T.: 'The Graves of Heitsi-eibib,' *Cape Monthly Magazine* XVI, pp. 259–65, 1878.

Hammond-Tooke, W. D.: 'The Symbolic Structure of Cape Nguni Cosmology' in *Religion and Social Change in Southern Africa*, edited by M. G. Whisson and M. West (London, 1975).

——— 'Do the South-Eastern Bantu Worship their Ancestors?' in *Social System and Tradition in Southern Africa*, edited by J. Argyle and E. Preston-Whyte (Cape Town, 1978).

Harinck, G.: 'Interaction between Xhosa and Khoi: Emphasis on the Period 1620–1750' in *African Societies in Southern Africa*, edited by L. Thompson (London, 1969).

Horton, R.: 'African Conversion,' *Africa* 41(2), pp. 85–108, 1971.

——— 'On the Rationality of Conversion,' *Africa* 45(3), pp. 219–35, and 45(4), pp. 373–99, 1975.

Lanham, L. W.: 'The proliferation and extension of Bantu phonemic systems influenced by Bushman and Hottentot,' *Proceedings of the Ninth International Congress of Linguistics*, Cambridge, Mass. 1962 (The Hague, 1964) pp. 382–91.

Mabona, M. A.: 'The Interaction and Development of different Religions in the Eastern Cape in the late Eighteenth and early Nineteenth Centuries, with Special Reference to the first two Xhosa Prophets' (Religious Studies Essay, School of Oriental and African Studies, University of London, 1973).

Maingard, L. F.: 'The Linguistic Approach to South African Prehistory and Ethnology,' *South African Journal of Science* XXXI, pp. 132–4, 1934.

Mafeje, A.: 'Religion, Class and Ideology in South Africa' in *Religion and Social Change in Southern Africa*, edited by M. G. Whisson and M. West (London and Cape Town, 1975).

McLaren, J.: 'Religious Beliefs and Superstitions of the Xhosa: A Study in Philology,' *South African Journal of Science* XV, pp. 418–24, 1918.

Nketia, J. H.: 'The Contribution of African Culture to Christian Worship,' *International Review of Missions* no. 187, July 1958.

Noyi, R. B.: 'Ama-Xosa History,' Appendix II in *Ntsikana: the Story of an African Convert* by J. K. Bokwe (Lovedale, 1914).

Nürnberger, K.: 'The Sotho Notion of the Supreme Being and the Impact of the Christian Proclamation,' *Journal of Religion in Africa* VII (fasc. 3), pp. 174–200, 1975.

Opland, J.: ' "Scop" and "Imbongi": Anglo-Saxon and Xhosa Traditional Poets,' *English Studies in Africa* 14, pp. 161–178, 1971.

———'Southeastern Bantu Eulogy and Early Indo-European Poetry,' *Research in African Literatures* II(3), pp. 295–307, Fall, 1980.

Ralston, R. D.: 'Xhosa Cattle Sacrifice, 1856–7: The Messianic Factor in African Resistance' in *Profiles in Self-Determination: African Responses to European Colonialism in Southern Africa 1652 – Present*, edited by D. Chanaiwa (Northridge, 1976) ch. 3.

Reyburn, H. A.: 'The Missionary as Rainmaker,' *The Critic* 1(8), pp. 146–53, 1933.

Ten Rhyne: 'A Short Account of the Cape of Good Hope and of the Hottentots who inhabit the Region (1686)' in *The Early Cape Hottentots*, edited by I. Schapera (Cape Town, 1933).

Theal, G. M.: 'Sparks from Kafir Anvils,' *Cape Monthly Magazine* n.s. 16, p. 191, 1878.

Van der Kemp, J. T.: Entries in Journal for 25 September 1799, 30 October and 2 November 1800, *Transactions of the Missionary Society* I, pp. 397, 427 (London, 1804).

———'An account of the religion, customs, . . . of Caffraria,' *Transactions of the Missionary Society* I, pp. 432–68. (London, 1804).

Van Wyk, J. A.: 'God: Near and Far. The Question of the Resting God in Africa,' *Theologia Viatorum* I(1), pp. 28–38, November 1973.

Van Warmelo, N. J.: 'A Tale of a Heap of Stones,' *Africana Notes and News* 16, pp. 278–83, 1964–5.

Wanger, W.: 'The Zulu Notion of God; according to the traditional Zulu God-names,' *Anthropos* 18–19(4–6), pp. 656–87, 1923–4; 20(3–4), pp. 558–78, 1925; 21(3–4), pp. 351–385, 1926.

Warner, J. C.: 'Notes' in *A Compendium of Kafir Laws and Customs*, compiled by J. MacLean (Cape Town, 1866).

Waters, H. T.: Evidence, *G.66–'83, Report on Proceedings with Appendices on the Government Commission on Native Laws and Customs*, 1883, p. 358.

Westphal, E. O. J.: 'The Linguistic Prehistory of Southern Africa: Bush, Kwadi, Hottentot, and Bantu Linguistic Relationships,' *Africa* 33(3), pp. 237–65, 1963.

Wilson, M.: 'The Early History of the Transkei and Ciskei,' *African Studies* 18(4), pp. 168–76, 1959.

———'The Nguni People' in *The Oxford History of South Africa* I, edited by M. Wilson and L. Thompson (Oxford, 1969) pp. 75–130.

V Oral evidence

Taped interviews with the following informants:

Chief S. M. Burns-Ncamashe, KwaGwali, Ciskei, 25 October 1978 and 18 February 1979.

Father A. Fischer, McKay's Nek, Transkei, 5 August 1981.

Prof V. Z. Gitywa, Department of Social Anthropology, University of Fort Hare, Ciskei, 17 July 1979.

Mr M. Hirst, Kaffrarian Museum, King William's Town, Cape Province, 26 May 1981.

Rev C. C. M. D. Hoyana, East London, Cape Province, 5 August 1979.

Father H. Kuckertz, Lumko Institute, Transkei, 17 October 1981.

Mr H. Nabe, Dean of Students, University of Fort Hare, Ciskei, 19 October 1979.

Prof H. W. Pahl, Director of the Xhosa Dictionary Project, University of Fort Hare, Ciskei, 13 July 1979.

Prof Z. S. Qangule, Department of Xhosa and Sotho, University of Fort Hare, Ciskei, 25 October 1978 and 16 July 1979.

Mr A. M. S. Sityana, Xhosa Dictionary Project, University of Fort Hare, Ciskei, 16 July 1979.

Mr M. Somhlahlo, Department of Social Science, University of Fort Hare, Ciskei, 25 October 1978.

Prof M. Wilson, Hogsback, Cape Province, 20 July 1979.

INDEX

satanic figure (see also umTyholi): 34, 95

Sawyer, H.: 46

Schapera, I.: 68

'Search Stage': 10, 66

Semitic religions: 17, 35

Shaw, W.: 43–4, 51, 76–7, 94

Sikhomo (Chief): 7

Soga, J. H.: 20–1, 44, 52

Soga, T.: 20, 34

sorcery: 32, 76, 96

St. John's River: 71, 83

St. Mark's district (Transkei): 67

Stavenisse (ship): 18

Steedman, A.: 25

storms see lightning

Stow, G. W.: 23

supreme being: 26, 32–3, 35, 41, 47, 62, 64–6, 68, 78–82, 85, 87, 92, 94–5, 101–3, 105–6

Tambookie see Thembu

Theal, G.: 66, 70

Thembu, the: 6, 18–9, 23, 77; ritual: 80

thikoloshe: 32

Thixo/Thiko (god-name): 42, 55, 62–3, 66–7, 83–4, 91, 93–5, 101, 103; as Christian god-name: 63, 93–4, 103–4

thunder see lightning

Thuthula: 77

Tinkhanna see Van der Kemp, J. T.

Tiquoa (Hottentot god): 24

Transkei: 8, 68, 79–80, 96, 105–6

Tshaka: 105

Tshawe (chiefdom): 6

Tshekedi: 105

Tshiwo: 66

Tsui//Goab (Khoi national hero/ supreme being): 24, 63, 67–8, 91–3

Tsuni-//Goam see Tsui//Goab

Tuikwa: 92

Twa (Hottentot ancestor): 20

Tyholi: 91, 95–6

Tyler, J.: 80

uhlanga/umhlanga (see also Eluhla-

ngeni): 18–20, 22–3, 25–6, 45; as praise-name: 45–6, 51, 54, 62, 101

Ukqamata see Qamata

Ukqitela/Ukugqitela: 71–2

Umhlangayo: 55

UmKhotsho: 83

Umoya: 71–2

umtendeleko (ritual): 80

Umzimvubu (river): 94

Umz'omzima: 54

Unkulunkulu (god-name): 44–5

Untu (first chief): 25

Utabu: 53, 55

Van der Kemp, J. T.: 42, 49, 76, 92–3

umVelatanqi: 53

Wanger, W.: 44–6, 48–9, 52, 54

Warner, J. C.: 48

Waters, Rev. H. T.: 67

Weber, M.: 106

Wesleyville: 77

Westphal, E. O. J.: 6

white men: 20, 26–7, 41, 43, 72, 109

Wikar, J. H.: 23

Wilson, M.: 6, 66

witches & witchcraft: 32, 47, 49, 76, 96

Xamaba: 68

Xhosa, the: 3, 6–10, 18–20, 24–5, 70, 92–3, 96, 109

  burial rites: 37

  conception of 'supreme being': 3, et passim

  cosmology: 52–3

  culture: 11

  death-myths: 32–7

  genealogies: 6

  intermarriage: 7

  language: 8, 25, 42, 62

  law: 77

  literature: 77

  myths of origin: 3, 17–27, 44, 53, 101

  oral tradition: 4, 17–8, 25, 33, 44, 66, 78